YORK NOTES

KS2 ENGLISH SATS

COMPLETE REVISION & TEST PRACTICE

MIKE GOULD, KAMINI KHANDURI, JOANNA ROSS, ELIZABETH WALTER AND KATE WOODFORD

YORK PRESS
322 Old Brompton Road, London SW5 9JH
PEARSON EDUCATION LIMITED
Edinburgh Gate, Harlow,
Essex CM20 2JE, United Kingdom
Associated companies, branches and representatives throughout the world

First published 2018

10 9 8 7 6 5 4 3 2 1

ISBN 978–1–2922–3280–5

Illustrations on pages 80–81 by Jeff Anderson
Typeset by Ken Vail Graphic Design
Printed in Slovakia

Text credit: Extract from the poem 'Ducks' by F. W. Harvey reproduced by kind permission of Eileen Griffiths

Image credits: GardenProject/Shutterstock for page 6 bottom and elsewhere / Samantha Cheah/Shutterstock for page 7 middle / GardenProject/Shutterstock for page 8 top and elsewhere / IrinaK/Shutterstock for page 8 bottom / Firdaus Khaled/Shutterstock for page 9 top / rvlsoft/Shutterstock for page 12 top / Valeri Potapova/Shutterstock for page 13 top / GardenProject/Shutterstock for page 14 bottom / GardenProject/Shutterstock for page 14 bottom / junpinzon/Shutterstock for page 15 top / Bokeh Blur Background/Shutterstock for page 16 middle / Autobahn/Shutterstock for page 17 top / Alexander P/Shutterstock for page 19 bottom /carolemagnet/Open Clip Art for page 23 top / DStarky/Shutterstock for page 23 bottom / Tomasz Trojanowski/Shutterstock for page 24 middle / wentus/Shutterstock for page 24 bottom / Ravenash/Shutterstock for page 25 top / graphic-line/Shutterstock for page 25 bottom / Lars Kastilan/Shutterstock for page 26 middle / Oxlock/Shutterstock for page 27 middle / Triff/Shutterstock for page 27 bottom / graphic-line/Shutterstock for page 28 top / PixieMe/Shutterstock for page 28 middle / Art Alex/Shutterstock for page 29 top / sonia etchison/Shutterstock for page 29 bottom / Lorelyn Medina/Shutterstock for page 32 top / Elena Blokhina/Shutterstock for page 32 middle / Africa Studio/Shutterstock for 33 top / baibaz/Shutterstock for page 33 bottom / SpeedKingz/Shutterstock for page 34 top / Jason Stitt/Shutterstock for page 34 middle / 3Dsculptor/Shutterstock for page 34 bottom / GraphicsRF/Shutterstock for page 35 top / bulia/Shutterstock for page 35 bottom / Will Thomass/Shutterstock for page 36 middle / Andy Dean Photography/Shutterstock for page 36 bottom / stscheb/Shutterstock for page 37 top / Sarah2/Shutterstock for page 37 bottom / M. Unal Ozmen/Shutterstock for page 37 bottom / iko/Shutterstock for page 38 middle / Mix3r/Shutterstock for page 39 top / NataSnow/Shutterstock for page 39 middle / Visual Generation/Shutterstock for page 39 bottom / Tanongsak Sangthong/Shutterstock for page 40 top / Dean Drobot/Shutterstock for page 40 top / SpeedKingz/Shutterstock for page 41 middle / photographyfirm/Shutterstock for page 41 bottom / medesulda/Shutterstock for page 42 top / Wang LiQiang/Shutterstock for page 42 middle / bus 109/Shutterstock for page 43 top / Fanya/Shutterstock for page 43 top / Pres Panayotov/Shutterstock for page 46 top / artshock/Shutterstock for page 46 bottom / JUAWA/Shutterstock for page 47 top / Nadezda/Shutterstock for page 47 middle / panicattack/Shutterstock for page 48 top / panicattack/Shutterstock for page 48 bottom / Baronb/Shutterstock for page 49 top / Mark_and_Anna_Wilson/Shutterstock for page 49 bottom / Olga_Angelloz/Shutterstock for page 49 middle / DucMityagov/Shutterstock for page 50 top / Notionpic/Shutterstock for page 50 middle / baibaz/Shutterstock for page 51 top / Ondrej Demi/Shutterstock for page 51 middle / Africa Studio/Shutterstock for page 52 top / glitch/Open Clip Art for page 52 bottom / nicubunu/Open Clip Art for page 52 bottom / Daisy Daisy/Shutterstock for page 52 bottom / wiradana9/Shutterstock for page 53 middle / Marina BH/Shutterstock for page 53 bottom / vectorlab2D/Shutterstock for page 56 top / Aniwhite/Shutterstock for page 57 top / NotionPic/Shutterstock for page 57 middle / Tanapon Samphao/Shutterstock for page 58 top / asawinimages/Shutterstock for page 58 middle / Blueguy/Shutterstock for page 59 top / leonbul/Shutterstock for page 59 bottom / Volodymyr Burdiak/Shutterstock for page 62 top / sardez/Shutterstock for page 62 middle / Digital Storm/Shutterstock for page 63 top / tynyuk/Shutterstock for page 64 middle / gdvcom/Shutterstock for page 64 middle / Ken Benner/Shutterstock for page 65 middle / Sarawut Padungkwan/Shutterstock for page 65 middle / Ancher/Shutterstock for page 66 top / Dora Zett/Shutterstock for page 66 middle / brgfx/Shutterstock for page 67 top / Jemastock/Shutterstock for page 67 middle / Andrey Makurin/Shutterstock for page 68 top / kurban/Shutterstock for page 68 bottom / Castleski/Shutterstock for page 71 bottom / pozzipool/Shutterstock for page 75 / frantisekhojdysz/Shutterstock for page 75 top / Ethan Daniels/Shutterstock for page 75 bottom / pozzipool/Shutterstock for page 76 / Merla/Shutterstock for page 76 top /

CONTENTS

SECTION FOUR: YORK NOTES SATS PRACTICE PAPER

SECTION FIVE: ANSWERS AND GLOSSARY

Reading Paper

What's it all about?

Five things you need to know:

❶ The Key Stage 2 test paper for **Reading** tests your **reading skills**.

❷ The whole test lasts **ONE HOUR**.

❸ You are given **THREE texts** to read in the exam: these will include **fiction** and **non-fiction** texts, and sometimes a **poem**.

❹ You will answer questions on **all three texts**. There will be 11–14 **questions** on each text.

❺ The questions will be of **THREE** different types:

- **Short-answer questions:** for these, you will only need to write a word, phrase or very simple sentence

- **Longer answer questions:** for these, you need to explain in more detail

- **Selected-answer questions:** for these, you need to tick, draw lines or circle the correct answer

What skills are tested?

You will be tested on:

- **Finding** the correct **information**

- Explaining **word meanings**

- **Summarising** ideas (saying what a longer section of a text is about)

- Making **inferences** (working out more hidden meanings)

- **Finding evidence** (being able to find information in a text to support what you say)

- **Explaining** how **a writer creates an effect** or meaning through the **words and phrases** they use

- **Finding/explaining** links or **connections** in a text

- **Predicting** what might happen in a text

- **Making comparisons** (how texts, or parts of them, are the same or different)

If all of this seems challenging, don't worry! There are pages on every one of these skills in the section that follows! So read on!

Explain word meanings

❶ You might be asked to **find a word** in a text **with a similar meaning**.

For example:

Read this paragraph then answer the question.

> Lara entered the echoing cave. In the distance she could hear the sound of trickling water but she had to stop for a moment. It was so gloomy she could not see her way over the rocks. She was stuck.

Q: ***Find*** and ***copy one*** word that suggests that the cave was dark.　　　　Answer: *gloomy.*

❷ You might have to **explain the meaning** of a word or **choose** a word **closest** in meaning.

GET IT RIGHT!

- Look for a word that is **closest in meaning** to the given word ('dark').
- Find the **correct part** of the paragraph (the bit about the cave).
- It could be the **same type of word** ('dark' is an **adjective**).

For example:

Read the sentence then answer the question.

> They had all **deserted** her: no one knew or cared where she was and she was miles from anywhere.

Q: *Give the **meaning** of the word '**deserted**' in this sentence.*

GET IT RIGHT!

- Are there **clues in the word** itself? For example, '**desert**ed': the **root word** is 'desert' = a wild, empty place.
- Read the **rest of the sentence** to help you. Are there clues in the other words?

nobody stayed ↓　　　　this sounds cruel ↓

> They had all **deserted** her: no one knew or cared where she was and she was *miles from anywhere.*

↑ on her own somewhere?

- Don't mix the word up with similar ones. This has nothing to do with 'dessert'!

Which of these words would be **closest in meaning** to 'deserted'?

a) *abandoned*　　　b) *left*　　　c) *released*　　　d) *dumped*

It is so Hard

Find information

❶ You might be asked to **find information** in a text.

For example:

Read this paragraph then answer the question.

> Sophie hurried along the stormy, windswept street. Suddenly, a tiny ball of fur shot across her path: a minute kitten! Was it alive? She bent over and picked it up tenderly. She gasped: its fur was soaked through, and its head was ice cold. But, its little heart throbbed.

Q: *What did Sophie find while she was out in the storm?*

Answer: *a kitten.*

GET IT RIGHT!

- This is a **WHAT** question so you are looking for a **short** answer.
- Use the **clue words** in the question to help you (e.g. *'Sophie'*, *'find'*, *'out in the storm'*) by **scanning** the text for them.

❷ You might be asked to **find more than one thing**.

For example:

Q: *Write down **two** things that worry Sophie when she picks up the kitten.* its soaked puf and ice cold head. it was soactpuf

GET IT RIGHT!

- Write down the **correct number** of things.
- Make sure you give **only what has been asked** (no more, no less).
- Don't base your answers on your own personal knowledge.

Which one of these answers is best?

a) *it was a tiny ball, had soaked fur, and ice-cold head*

b) *its soaked fur and ice-cold head*

c) *its soaked fur, ice-cold head, and because kittens are vulnerable without their parents*

❸ You might be asked to find information to decide whether something is **true** or **false**.

- A **true** statement is one that is **correct**.
- A **false** statement is one that is **incorrect**.

For example:

Read this paragraph then answer the question.

Cats have played an important role in the history of the world. It is believed they were domesticated about 10,000 years ago. The ancient Egyptians worshipped a cat goddess called Bast or Bastet, and many cats and kittens were mummified and buried with their human owners. If you injured or killed a cat in Egyptian times you could be punished very severely indeed. In fact, the word 'cat' comes from Egypt as the North African word for it was 'quattah'.

Q: *Using information from the text, tick one box in each row to show whether the statement is **true** or **false**.*

Statement	True	False
Cats first became pets about 100,000 years ago.	✓	
The Egyptian cat goddess was called Bast or Bastet.	✓	
Cats were often buried with humans.	✓	
The word 'cat' comes from Ethiopia.		✓

GET IT RIGHT!

- **Read the statement carefully**. Then **find the part of the text** you need.
- If you need to find **a number** in the text, make sure it's the **correct** number **AND matches the statement**.
- Sometimes the statement will use **different wording** from the original text (e.g. 'derives' means 'comes from').
- **Check** the statement **against the text**. Does it say the same thing? If it does, then tick 'True'. If it doesn't, tick 'False'.

Don't be fooled by tiny differences between the questions and the text!

RATE YOUR PROGRESS!   'I can find the correct information in a text.'
I'm fine ▢   Look again 🔍 ▢   Ask an adult ❓ ▢

Summarise information and ideas

❶ You may be asked what the overall theme of a **paragraph or section of text** is.

For example:

Read the paragraphs then answer the question.

> Inactive lifestyles (e.g. watching <u>too much television</u> or spending <u>too long on our phones</u>) mean we are <u>not</u> <u>doing enough</u> to keep <u>healthy</u>. But it doesn't take much <u>exercise</u> to make things better.
>
> A short jog or bike ride can be <u>very enjoyable</u> – and <u>won't</u> <u>take up too much time</u>. Plan to fit <u>exercise</u> into your daily life and you will <u>love</u> the <u>health</u> benefits!
>
> Getting your heart rate up is one reason why exercise is important. It trains your body to move blood and oxygen to your muscles in an efficient way.

The key words and phrases are underlined to help you!

Q: *What is the **main message** about exercise?*

Which of these answers is best?

a) *We can all find time for a bit of exercise.*

b) *Everyone watches too much television.*

c) *Bike rides and jogging are great fun.*

The clues should tell you that c) is the answer.

GET IT RIGHT!

- Look for **repeated words** or **phrases**, e.g. *'health/healthy'* and *'exercise'*.
- Look for words or phrases that **show opinion**, e.g. *'too much television', 'very enjoyable', 'love … health benefits'*.
- Check the **first** and **last** sentences of the paragraph. These often **introduce** or **sum up** the topic.

❷ You may be asked to put paragraphs in order according to what each is about.

For example:

Q: ***Number*** *these summaries of the three paragraphs in the text above.*

A higher heart rate is good for us. ③

Our lifestyle has a lack of activity. ①

Brief exercise is fun and doesn't take up much time. ②

GET IT RIGHT!

- Read each paragraph carefully. Some may cover very similar information. Look for the **key words** and **any different or new pieces of information**.

RATE YOUR PROGRESS! 'I can summarise information correctly.'

I'm fine ▢ Look again 🔍 ▢ Ask an adult ❓ ▢

Make inferences

❶ You might be asked to work out the meaning of something in a text.

Writers do not always say things directly, but **suggest** ideas instead. You need to **infer** (read **between** the lines) what the writer means by looking at **clues** in the text.

For example:

> Jo was reluctant to take part in the race. ⟵——— tells us clearly that Jo does not want to race
>
> Jo slowly put on her running shoes. She kept glancing at her watch – only five minutes. She felt a horrible sick feeling in her belly.

⟵ shows her acting reluctantly

⟵ her feelings tell us her thoughts

All these clues help us **infer** that Jo does not want to take part in the race.

Now read the following sentence then answer the question.

> Jo's legs trembled as she began the race against the older, bigger girls: she felt completely out of her depth.

Q: *Explain **what is suggested** by the phrase **out of her depth** in the sentence below.* *I think it's because Jo was scared.*

GET IT RIGHT!

- Check the **other information** in the sentence: 'legs *trembled*', '*began the race*', '*older, bigger* girls'. You tremble when you are nervous or afraid. A race is a competition where others want to beat you. 'Older, bigger girls' means Jo is younger and smaller, so she might not be as fast or strong.
- Now **check the phrase** itself: '*out of her depth*'. This means when you're in water but can't touch the bottom. It can make you feel scared.

The answer could be: *Jo didn't feel confident in her ability to race the other girls.*

❷ You might be given an inference question that asks 'what'.

For example:

Read the text then answer the question.

> Jess tried to smile at her friend Shahena but she just couldn't – the taste of the uncooked burger clung to her mouth. What could she say?
>
> 'I'm so full,' she said, patting her stomach, which was rumbling a little.

11

As Shahena glanced away for a moment, Jess hid the limp salad under her burger bun. She took a sip of her drink – at least that was refreshing and tasty. It had been so kind of her friend to treat her to the meal. Perhaps the birthday cake Shahena had ordered would be better.

Q: **What** are **three** ways Jess shows she is not enjoying her meal?

GET IT RIGHT!

- Writers **don't** always say exactly what they mean. Sometimes we need to look at what a character **says and does** to work out what is happening.
- Focus on the clues in the question (e.g. *'three ways'* and *'Jess shows'*. This means you must look for things **Jess does** and the way **she looks/behaves**.)

Things to look for	Example	Inference
What she says	*'I'm so full'*	How does this show Jess is not enjoying the meal?
What she does	*'Jess tried to smile'*	This is a lie – her stomach is *'rumbling'* so she is still hungry.
What she does	*'Jess hid the limp salad under her burger bun'*	

What does the example in the last row tell you?

❸ You might be asked an **inference question** that asks 'why'.

For example:

Q: *Why doesn't Jess want Shahena to know she is* **not** *enjoying the meal?*

Watch out for evidence that **doesn't support** the statement, such as Jess enjoying her drink!

GET IT RIGHT!

- Check the rest of the text to work out more about the situation: Shahena is Jess's friend (*'her friend Shahena'*) and it's Jess's birthday (*'the birthday cake Shahena had ordered'*). These clues show Jess likes Shahena and Shahena is a kind person.

Answer: *Jess didn't want to upset Shahena as she had been so kind to buy her the meal.*

RATE YOUR PROGRESS!   'I can infer meanings from clues in a text.'
I'm fine ☐   Look again 🔍 ☐   Ask an adult ☐

Find evidence and identify facts and opinions

❶ You might be asked to find information which supports a statement or point.

For example:

Read this paragraph then answer the question.

> Businessman Sir Alan Sugar is worth approximately one billion pounds. However, he once sold goods out of a van he had bought for £50. He paid for the van by withdrawing all the money he had saved (just £100) from his Post Office account. Now, he even owns his own aeroplane!

Q: *Sir Alan Sugar wasn't always a wealthy man. Give **one piece of evidence** from the text that supports this.*

GET IT RIGHT!

- Look for references to Sir Alan being wealthy/rich or references to money.
- Decide whether this information **does or does not** support the statement.

Example	Meaning	Does or does not support the statement
'worth approximately one billion pounds'	This doesn't say whether he has always had a billion pounds or not.	Does not support the statement.
'a van he had bought for £50'	The van was cheap but this doesn't say whether he was rich or poor.	Does not support the statement.
'all the money he had saved (just £100)'	This was all he had and £100 is not a lot of money.	Does support the statement.

Answer: *The text says he withdrew 'all the money he had saved which was £100', which shows he didn't have much at that time.*

❷ You might be asked to explain something and then support it with evidence.

'I'd feel rich if I had £50!'

Read the paragraph then answer the question.

> Rosie raced like a greyhound to get to the ball first, and then cleverly noticed the goalkeeper off her line. Before the keeper could get back, Rosie kicked the ball over the keeper's head and into the empty net.

Q: *How is the girl in the story made to seem talented?*

Explain two ways, giving evidence from the text to support your answer.

GET IT RIGHT!

- There are often **several marks** for this type of question so check **how many** pieces of evidence/clues you need to give. The first way could be:

*The writer describes how fast she is **by using the phrase 'like a greyhound'**.*

(the way)   (the evidence)

Can you find the second way and evidence to support it?

❸ You might be asked whether something is a **fact or opinion**.

For example:

Q: *Re-read the text on Sir Alan Sugar. Which of the following are **facts** and which are **opinions**?*

	Fact	Opinion
He had a van worth £50.	✓	
He is the most successful businessman ever.		✓
He is worth about one billion pounds.	✓	

GET IT RIGHT!

- Check if a statement is **backed up by evidence or figures** (e.g. dates, measurements, statistics). If it is, it is probably a **fact**. For example, 'Germany won the World Cup in 2014.' is a fact. It cannot be argued with – lots of people saw it happen!
- Check if someone says what they **think or believe**. This is an **opinion**. For example, 'Germany is the best football team in the world.' is an **opinion**. Some people might think a different team is.
- **Facts** are often **used to back up opinions**. For example:

*I think Germany is the best team in the world **because** they won the World Cup in 2014.*

(fact)   (opinion)

I think England is the best team in the world.

That definitely *is* an opinion!

RATE YOUR PROGRESS!   'I can find evidence to support a statement or a point.'

I'm fine ■   Look again 🔍 ■   Ask an adult ❓ ■

14

❶ You might be asked to **predict what might happen next** in a text or to **explain why** you think someone **will act** in a particular way.

For example:

Read this text then answer the question.

> It was a week to go to the show. Sherri still hadn't practised her song, and was sitting around feeling sorry for herself. Her brother came into her room.
>
> 'What are you doing? You need to practise!'
>
> 'I can't. I'm too nervous – and I'll be terrible anyway!'
>
> 'Come on!' he told her. 'I'll help.'
>
> Sherri reluctantly followed him into his room. 'Look – I'll play the guitar bit – and you just sing. He started playing and, after a few chords, Sherri joined in. Her voice wobbled a bit, but she slowly gained in confidence. Perhaps she wasn't so bad after all?

Q: *Do you think Sherri will **enjoy** the talent show?*

Yes ☑   No ◯   Maybe ◯

*Explain your choice **fully**, giving **evidence** from the text.*

GET IT RIGHT!

- Read what is happening in the text **as a whole**. At first, Sherri doesn't even want to practise (e.g. *'still hadn't practised her song'*), but then things change. Can you find other evidence for this stage?
- Check for **changes** or how a character or situation **develops** (e.g. *'Her voice wobbled a bit'*, then her opinion starts to change, *'she slowly gained in confidence. Perhaps she wasn't so bad after all?'*)
- Make a decision based on what is **probably** going to happen.

Answer: *Maybe. It does not say that Sherri is enjoying or looking forward to the show. At first she says she's 'too nervous' and will be 'terrible'. However, at the end she admits she isn't 'so bad'.*

RATE YOUR PROGRESS!   'I can predict what is going to happen in a text.'

I'm fine ☀ ☑   Look again 🔍 ▢   Ask an adult ❓ ▢

I have done this it is easy.

Explain structure

❶ You might be asked to explain what a **part of the text does**.

Here are six parts of a story about Count Otto and what each part does.

Quotations	Purpose/function (what it does)
'The castle walls loomed down'	1 To describe **setting**
'Count Otto looked kind but was evil'	2 To introduce or describe a **character**
'Otto leapt onto his horse'	3 To show **action**
'Otto changed five years ago'	4 To show **past events**, give a **flashback**
'A year later, Otto was finally released'	5 To show **later events, flashforward**
'Be careful who you trust'	6 To give a **moral or lesson**

Q: *Match each of the quotations below with **one** of the functions 1–6 above. Write the correct number for each quotation.*

a) *Lily kicked open the door, and slithered down the rope.* ④

b) *The river shone and sparkled a hundred feet below her.* ①

c) *It was dangerous, but Lily was determined.* ③

d) *She remembered those swimming lessons in the big lake when she'd been five.* ②

❷ You might be asked to **find an important point or change** in a text.

For example:

Read the paragraph then answer the question.

Lily swam steadily down the long, broad river. She felt very relieved. She had left evil Count Otto behind and soon she would be back in her parents' cottage, eating warm soup by a blazing fire. She turned her head to her right to take a breath, and that's when, to her horror, she saw him. Otto! He was racing along by the side of the river bank on his black horse. Soon the river reached a waterfall and she would have to get out. And Otto would be waiting.

Q: *Where does the mood change? Find and copy the words that show the change.* Horror

GET IT RIGHT!

- Scan sections of the text quickly to get the general idea of what is going on.
- Then look for positive or negative mood words or phrases that show a change in feelings (e.g. *'felt very relieved'* = positive but *'to her horror'* = negative).

RATE YOUR PROGRESS!   'I can explain how a text's structure works.'

I'm fine ☀ ☑   Look again 🔍 ☑   Ask an adult ❓ ☑

Explain language choice

❶ You might be asked to explain what **effect** a **writer's choice of language** has.

For example:

Read the sentence then answer the question.

> The woman's hand was like an old map.

Q: *What does this description **suggest** about the woman's hand?*

GET IT RIGHT!

- Look carefully at the given words.
- Consider what other words or ideas might **describe the same thing** (e.g. 'lined', 'worn', 'creased' might describe an old map).
- Decide which of your words or ideas fit the thing described.

Answer: *It suggests the woman's hand is worn and creased with lines.*

Now answer a similar question:

Q: *The fog was a cloak that shielded them from the enemy.*

*Give **two** impressions this gives you of the fog.*

❷ You might be asked to find **words or phrases** that **describe things** in a specific way.

For example:

Read the paragraph then answer the question.

> The flowers in the forest were bursting with vivid colours. Through the trees, a pure blue lake shimmered in the light. Perfect ripples spread from the middle as rain began to fall. A nearby parrot squawked loudly, disturbing the peace, but soon it was silent again. Mist hovered round the edges of the lake like a lovely silver necklace.

Q: *Find and copy **four** words or phrases from the text that make the lake seem beautiful.*

shimmered, ripples, vivid and lovely

GET IT RIGHT!

- Write down the **correct number** of examples even if there are more to choose from.
- Choose words which are **similar or close in meaning** to what you have been asked to identify (e.g. *'pure'*, *'shimmered'*, *'perfect ripples'*, *'mist... like a lovely silver necklace'* could all be beautiful).
- Make sure you write about **only what has been asked** – nothing else.

Make comparisons

❶ You might be asked in what ways things or people change.

For example:

Read the paragraph then answer the question.

> As Sherri waited to go on stage she fiddled (nervously) with her microphone. Sweat prickled her forehead and her hands felt clammy. She paced around, her heart thumping. Then she heard her name called. (Suddenly the nerves seemed to disappear.) A calm, controlled feeling flooded her body. She was going to do this. It would be ok.

GET IT RIGHT!

- Make sure you **only read the section mentioned**. You might be given the page or paragraph number.
- Check what the thing or person is like at the start. **What has changed** by the end?

Q: **How** does Sherri's mood **change** as she waits at the talent show?

❷ You might be asked to compare how two things are similar or different.

For example:

Read the text then answer the question.

> In the UK, although the red squirrel is a native species, the grey squirrel is the more dominant of the two types. It is slightly larger, and is originally a native of North America. It is everywhere in the UK, numbering about 2½ million unlike the red which numbers only about 15,000. Introduced around the year 1870, grey squirrels also carry a virus which they are immune to, but the red squirrel is not.

GET IT RIGHT!

- Check for comparative adjectives, such as 'more', 'smaller', 'greater'.
- Check for words/phrases that **show difference**, e.g. 'in contrast', 'but'.
- Identify **things that can be compared** (e.g. appearance – 'grey'/'red').

Q: *How are the red and grey squirrels **different**?*

Fill in this grid with correct information about the two types of squirrel.

	Grey squirrel	Red squirrel
Native of?		
Numbers		
Health		

Ducks

From troubles of the world I turn to ducks,
Beautiful comical things
Sleeping or curled
Their heads beneath white wings
By water cool,
Or finding curious things
To eat in various mucks
Beneath the pool,
Tails uppermost, or waddling
Sailor-like on the shores
Of ponds, or paddling
– Left! Right! – with fanlike feet
Which are for steady oars
When they (white galleys) float
Each bird a boat
Rippling at will the sweet
Wide waterway...
When night is fallen you creep
Upstairs, but drakes and **dillies**
Nest with pale water-stars,
Moonbeams and shadow bars,
And water-lilies:
Fearful too much to sleep
Since they've no locks
To click against the teeth
Of weasel and fox.
And warm beneath
Are eggs of cloudy green
Whence hungry rats and lean
Would stealthily suck
New life, but for the **mien**
The bold ferocious mien
Of the mother-duck.

By F. W. Harvey

Note: The above is an extract from the longer poem.

GLOSSARY

dillies – female ducks

mien – a person's or animal's appearance or manner that shows how they are feeling

❶ *From troubles of the world, I turn to ducks*
Beautiful comical things

Which word is closest in meaning to the word '<u>comical</u>'?

Tick **one**.

colourful ☐

feathered ☐

funny ☑

cute ☐

_____
1 mark

❷ Look at the two lines beginning: *Left! Right!*

The poet compares the duck's feet to which piece of boating equipment?

_____ oars _____

_____
1 mark

❸ ... with *<u>fanlike feet</u>*

Here the poet uses alliteration (words that start with the same sound) to describe the duck's feet. Find and copy another example of alliteration in the poem.

_____ Wide water way _____

_____
1 mark

❹ What three animals does the writer mention as a threat to the duck or her eggs?

1. _rats_
2. _~~ducks~~_ ✗ _mien_
3. _fox_ ✗

_____
1 mark

❺ Look at the four lines beginning: *Fearful too much to sleep.*

Why are the ducks afraid of going to sleep?

~~fox~~ animals can kill ~~them~~. ✗

fox rats mien

_____
1 mark

❻ Number the information below 1–4 to show the order in which it is given in the poem.

a description of how ducks swim ③

a description of the threats from predators ④ ✗

a description of when ducks sleep ① ✗ 3

a description of how ducks eat ②

_____
1 mark

❼ This poem suggests that the poet likes ducks. Find two adjectives in the poem that support this.

rippling at will the ~~sweete~~

_____

_____
2 marks

Grammar, punctuation and vocabulary (Paper 1)

What's it all about?

Four things you need to know:

❶ Paper 1 of your Key Stage 2 **English Grammar, Punctuation and Spelling** SATs tests your **knowledge** of grammar, punctuation and vocabulary.

❷ The whole test lasts **45 MINUTES**.

❸ There will be up to **50 questions** and 50 marks in total.

❹ The questions will be of **TWO** different types:

- **Multiple-choice answer questions:** for these, you will only need to tick, draw a line or circle the correct answer

- **Short-answer questions:** for these, you will need to write a word, a few words or a sentence on the line or in the box provided

What skills are tested?

You will be tested on:

- **Identifying word types and classes** (nouns, pronouns, verbs, determiners, adjectives, adverbs, prepositions)

- **Understanding sentence grammar and verb tenses** (sentence types and forms, subject and object, phrases, clauses, conjunctions, modal verbs, active and passive, standard and non-standard English, formal and informal language)

- **Using punctuation correctly** (sentence punctuation, commas, inverted commas, brackets, dashes and hyphens, colons and bullet points, semi-colons, apostrophes)

- **Understanding vocabulary and using it correctly** (prefixes, suffixes, word families, synonyms and antonyms)

If all of this seems challenging, don't worry! There are pages on every one of these skills in the section that follows! So read on!

Nouns

You might be asked to identify a **noun** in a sentence.

For example:

Q: *Circle all the **nouns** in the sentence below.*

The (girls) were eating (toast) in the (kitchen).

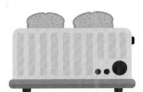

> A **noun** is a type of **word class**. A word class is a group of words that all do the same thing in a sentence.

GET IT RIGHT!

- **Nouns** are the words we use for **naming things** – all the things you can see, feel, hear, taste and smell.
- Ordinary things, such as 'table' or 'cat', are **common nouns**. **Common nouns** start with a **lower case letter**.
- Names for things like people, places, days and months are **proper nouns**. Remember that **proper nouns** start with a **capital letter** (*Harry Potter*, *Spain*, *Monday*, *December*).

Collective nouns

A **collective noun** is a noun that refers to a **group** of people or animals. Words like 'family' and 'team' are collective nouns.

An army of ants

A class of students

A flock of seagulls

Concrete nouns and abstract nouns

Concrete nouns are things that really exist, such as 'potato', 'bed' or 'plane'.

Abstract nouns are things that you think about or feel, such as 'love', 'truth' or 'anger'.

love   anger   sadness   friendship

GET IT RIGHT!

- If you **can see** or touch something, it's probably a **concrete noun**.
- If you **can't see** or touch something, it's probably an **abstract noun**.

RATE YOUR PROGRESS!   'I can identify different types of noun.'

I'm fine   Look again   Ask an adult

Pronouns

You might be asked to use a **pronoun** in a sentence.

For example:

Q: *Replace the underlined word or words in each sentence with the correct **pronoun**.*

a) *When Joe got home, <u>Joe</u> was hungry.*　　✔ he

b) *Joe went to the fridge and opened <u>the fridge</u>.*　　✔ it

Possessive pronouns

A **possessive pronoun** is a **pronoun** that shows who **owns** something.

That's not yours – it's mine!

It's not ours – it's hers!

Relative pronouns

A **relative pronoun** is a **pronoun** that **joins** two parts of a sentence that have connected information. Examples include 'which', 'that' or 'who'.

GET IT RIGHT!

- **Pronouns** are words that we use to **replace** nouns, e.g. 'it'.
- **Personal pronouns** are words, such as 'I', 'me', 'they' and 'them', that we use so that we don't have to repeat the names of people and things we have already mentioned.
  ✔ *When Clara saw her friends, she ran to meet them.*
  ✘ *When Clara saw her friends, Clara ran to meet her friends.*
- Remember to use **'I'** and not **'me'** for **doing things**:
  ✔ *My mum and I like going shopping.*
  ✘ *My mum and me like going shopping.*

GET IT RIGHT!

- A **relative pronoun** often tells us more about a person or thing:
  This is my friend who you met at the beach.
  Here's the apple that I picked.
- You can use **relative pronouns** to make two sentences into one:
  We had fish and chips. That's my favourite dinner.
  We had fish and chips, which is my favourite dinner.

RATE YOUR PROGRESS!　　'I can use pronouns in sentences.'

I'm fine ☐　　Look again 🔍 ☐　　Ask an adult ❓ ☐

Determiners

You might be asked to identify a **determiner** in a sentence.

For example:

Q: *Circle all the **determiners** in the sentence below.*

I saw (an) alligator in (a) pond when I went to (the) zoo.

GET IT RIGHT!

- **Determiners** are words that go **before** nouns. They **give you information** about the **noun**.
- **Articles** are a type of **determiner** we use all the time: 'a', 'an', 'the'.
- Remember to use **'a'** before a word that starts with a **consonant** (*a sunny day, a pizza*) and **'an'** before a word that starts with a **vowel** (*an idea, an ostrich*).

Different determiners

You use some **determiners** to say which person or thing you are talking about:

this baby	*these glasses*	*that flower*	*those birds*

You use some **determiners** to say how much or how many you mean:

some cake	*enough money*	*any friends*

Another group of **determiners** shows who something belongs to:

my father	*your house*	*her school*	*our breakfast*

Numbers are **determiners** too:

five pounds	*twelve days*	*twenty minutes*

GET IT RIGHT!

- Make sure you don't confuse **determiners** (*my, your, her, our*) with **possessive pronouns** (*mine, yours, hers, ours*).
- Remember that to show who something belongs to, you use 'your' and not 'you're' (*It's your party today!*).

Verbs

You might be asked to identify a **verb** in a sentence.

For example:

Q: *Which sentence uses the word <u>touch</u> as a **verb**?*

a) *He felt a light <u>touch</u> on his shoulder.*

b) *Can you <u>touch</u> your toes?*

c) *We lost <u>touch</u> years ago.*

Answer: b) – touch is an action here.

Verb tenses

Verbs have different forms, called **tenses**, which tell you **when** an action happened.

Tense	Example
The **past** tense tells you something **happened**.	*I brushed my hair.*
The **present** tense tells you something **happens now**.	*I brush my hair.*
The **future** tense tells you something **will happen**.	*I will brush my hair.*

Subjects and verbs agree

The **subject** is the person or thing that **does** the **verb**. When a **verb** is in the right form for its **subject**, we say that the **subject** and **verb** **agree**.

Helping verbs

A **helping verb** is an extra **verb** that **goes with the main verb** in a sentence.

Sometimes the **helping verb** **changes the tense** of the **verb** (*I have broken my leg*).

Sometimes it **changes the meaning** of the sentence (*They might come and visit us*).

Adjectives

You might be asked to identify an **adjective** in a sentence.

For example:

Q: *Which sentence uses the word* <u>right</u> *as an* **adjective**?

a) *She looked left and* <u>right</u>.

b) *I used my* <u>right</u> *hand.*

c) <u>Right</u> *is the opposite of wrong.*

d) *You have no* <u>right</u> *to enter this building.*

Answer: b) – right describes the hand here.

GET IT RIGHT!

- **Adjectives** are words that we use to **describe** people and things (a *blue* car).
- **Adjectives** can be simple words, such as 'hot' and 'small', or more unusual words, such as 'aggressive'.
- Remember that **adjectives** sometimes go **before** a **noun** (*Is that a new <u>skateboard</u>?*) and sometimes **after** a **verb** (*It <u>is</u> new*).

Adjectives for comparing

Comparative adjectives are used for comparing two things (*Autumn is colder than summer*).

Superlative adjectives are used for comparing more than two things (*Winter is the coldest season of the year*).

GET IT RIGHT!

- To turn a **short** adjective into a **comparative adjective**, we generally add 'er' to the end of the word (*I am tall but you are taller*).
- To turn a **short** adjective into a **superlative adjective**, we generally add 'the' before the word and 'est' to the end of the word (*She is the tallest*).
- Remember that with a **longer** adjective,
  – we put the word 'more' before it to make a comparative **adjective** (*It's more expensive*)
  – we put the words 'the most' before it to make a superlative **adjective** (*It's the most expensive*).

RATE YOUR PROGRESS! **'I can identify adjectives in sentences.'**

I'm fine ☀ ▢   Look again 🔍 ▢   Ask an adult ❓ ▢

Adverbs

You might be asked to identify an **adverb** in a sentence.

For example:

Q: *Circle the **adverb** in the sentence below.*

Harry walked (quickly) because he was late for school.

GET IT RIGHT!

- **Adverbs** are words that **add information** about **verbs**. They tell you **how** someone does something.
- Generally, an **adverb** is made up of the **adjective** with 'ly' on the end (*loud–loudly*).
- There are different types of **adverb**, explained below.

Adverbs with adjectives

Not all **adverbs** tell you about **verbs**. Some **adverbs** come **before** adjectives. The **adverb** makes the meaning of the **adjective** weaker or stronger.

You're so clever.　　　　*She's very kind.*

I'm really late.　　　　*It's quite cold.*

Adverbs of possibility

We use **adverbs of possibility** to say how sure we are about something.

Perhaps it will rain tomorrow.

You probably don't like spinach.

Adverbials

Sometimes we use a **group of words** as an **adverb**. This is called an **adverbial**, or an **adverbial phrase**.

She walked as fast as she could.

A **fronted adverbial** is an **adverb** or **adverbial phrase** at the beginning of a sentence.

Later that day, I heard the bad news.

GET IT RIGHT!

- We usually **put a comma after a fronted** adverbial.
  Before you start, sharpen your pencil.
- If the **adverbial phrase** is not at the beginning, you don't use a **comma**.
  Sharpen your pencil before you start.

Adverbs of time and place

Adverbs of time tell us **when** a thing happens (*See you soon*).

Adverbs of place tell us **where** a thing happens (*We went there*).

Prepositions

You might be asked to identify a **preposition** in a sentence.

For example:

Q: *Circle all the* **prepositions** *in the sentence below.*

Dad stayed (at) home but I went (to) the park (with) Mum.

GET IT RIGHT!

- **Prepositions** are little words that usually come **before** nouns.
- **Prepositions** **of place** tell you **where** something is (*in the bath; above the clouds*), or the direction in which it is moving (*from Oxford; down the stairs*).
- **Prepositions** **of time** tell you **when** something happens (*after lunch*), or for how long it happens (*till the morning*).

Two-word prepositions

Most **prepositions** are single words but some are made up of more than one word. Some of these are **prepositions** **of cause** – they tell you **why** something happened (*due to; because of*).

Omar sat next to Ella.

There was snow on top of the mountain.

They didn't go out because of the rain.

I had a lovely birthday thanks to Molly.

Here are some common prepositions:

by	under	without
on	below	between
	before	over

Prepositions before pronouns

Prepositions can come **before** pronouns as well as before **nouns**.

They went to the cinema without <u>*him*</u>.

Ben was behind <u>*me*</u> *in the queue.*

The dog sat between <u>*them*</u>.

GET IT RIGHT!

- Remember that **pronouns** are words like 'me', 'you', 'him' and 'them'. You can use them **instead of** nouns.

RATE YOUR PROGRESS!   'I can identify prepositions in sentences.'

I'm fine ☐   Look again 🔍 ☐   Ask an adult ❓ ☐

SATs practice: Word types/classes

❶ What is the **word class** of the underlined word in the sentence below?

The test was <u>really</u> difficult but he tried to finish it.

Tick one.

adjective ☐

determiner ☐

verb ☐

adverb ☐

_____

1 mark

❷ Circle the **possessive pronouns** in the passage below.

When we arrived at the hotel, Mum told us which room was ours. The bed by the window was mine and my sister had the bed by the door.

_____

1 mark

❸ Which **two** sentences contain a **preposition**?

Tick two.

Charlie is sitting behind his friend. ☐

She asked you to come outside. ☐

I'll be there at six tomorrow. ☐

My teacher helps me when I get stuck. ☐

_____

1 mark

4 Circle the **relative pronoun** in the sentence below.

Have you seen the book that I was reading?

_____

1 mark

5 Draw a line to match each sentence to the correct **determiner**. Use each determiner only **once**.

Sentence	Determiner

I've got ____ new baby sister.

the

I used to be ____ only child.

a

Being a big brother is ____ best thing.

an

_____

1 mark

Challenge yourself!

Was that all too easy? Challenge yourself with one final, tricky question!

6 Which sentence uses the word <u>cover</u> as a **verb**?

Tick **one**.

My duvet <u>cover</u> is blue and red. ☐

That's a <u>cover</u> of a Beatles' song. ☐

I'll <u>cover</u> the table with a pretty cloth. ☐

She read her new book from <u>cover</u> to <u>cover</u>. ☐

_____

1 mark

Sentence functions

> You might be asked to identify different sentence functions.

For example:

Q: *Which sentence must end with a* ***question mark?***

a) *What a lovely day it is*

b) *What goes up must come down*

c) *Tell me what to do next*

d) *What food do cats like best*

Answer: d) – it's asking a question.

Types of sentence

A **statement** tells you something. It ends with a **full stop**.

I've bought a new hat.

An **exclamation** shows strong feelings. It starts with 'What' or 'How', and ends with an **exclamation mark**. Exclamations can be very short and they **don't always have a** **verb**.

What a ridiculous hat!

How silly you look in it!

A **question** asks something. It ends with a **question mark**.

Why are you wearing that hat?

A **command** tells someone to do something. **Commands** usually start with a **verb** and end with a **full stop**. Urgent **commands** end with an **exclamation mark**.

Take it off!

Go and buy another hat.

GET IT RIGHT!

- **Sentences have different functions** – to make a **statement**, express an emotion, ask a **question** or tell someone to do something.
- A sentence always **starts** with a **capital letter** and **ends** with a **full stop**, a **question mark** or an **exclamation mark**.
- Most sentences have a **verb**.
- Remember that a sentence must make sense on its own.

> Who...?
> What...?
> Where...?
> When...?
> Which...?
> How?

GET IT RIGHT!

- You can turn a **statement** into a **question** by adding a **question tag**. Don't forget to put a **comma** before a **question tag**.
  My hat suits me, doesn't it?
  You are joking, aren't you?

RATE YOUR PROGRESS! 'I can identify different sentence functions.'

I'm fine ☐   Look again 🔍 ☐   Ask an adult ☐

Clauses

You might be asked to identify different types of clause.

For example:

Q: *Circle the **main clause** in each sentence below.*

a) (She did well in the competition,) despite feeling tired.

b) *If you don't need it,* (give it to a charity shop.)

c) *Although they love dogs,* (they chose a cat.)

Main clauses

Main clauses **make sense on their own** (*I like football. My brother likes swimming*).

If you have two or more **main clauses**…

YOU CAN

- write them as **two separate sentences:**
  I like football. My brother likes swimming.
- **join** them together into one sentence **with a conjunction** such as 'and', 'but', or 'so':
  I like football but my brother likes swimming.

YOU CAN'T

- **run them together** with no **conjunction:**
  I like football my brother likes swimming.

- **put a comma** between the **clauses:**
  I like football, my brother likes swimming.

Subordinate clauses

A **subordinate clause** **doesn't make sense on its own**. It **must be joined** to a **main clause**.

My brother likes swimming although he isn't very good.

I am going to bed when I've finished my homework.

If you like chocolate, you can share mine.

RATE YOUR PROGRESS!   'I can identify different types of clause.'

I'm fine ☀ ▢   Look again 🔍 ▢   Ask an adult ❓ ▢

Phrases

You might be asked to identify a **phrase**.

For example:

Q: *Circle the **phrase** in the sentence below.*

The boys walked (very slowly.)

GET IT RIGHT!

- **Phrases** are **groups of words that give us information**, but they aren't a whole **clause**.
- In a **phrase**, there may be no **subject**, no **verb**, or neither a **subject** nor a **verb**.
  The girls dance happily and energetically.
  In the city, it's always hot.
  The train travelled at lightning speed.
  I love living near the sea.

Noun phrases

We use **noun phrases** to **add information about** nouns without using lots of sentences. **Noun phrases** can be different lengths depending on how much information you want to give.

Beatrice was watching a good film.

Beatrice was watching a good film about pirates.

Beatrice was watching a good film about funny pirates.

Beatrice was watching a good film about funny pirates in the Caribbean.

RATE YOUR PROGRESS!   'I can identify phrases and noun phrases.'

I'm fine ☐   Look again 🔍 ☐   Ask an adult ❓ ☐

Subject and object

You might be asked to identify **subjects** and **objects**.

For example:

Q: *Circle the **object** in the sentence below.*

Next week, I am taking (Jack) to the seaside.

GET IT RIGHT!

- The **subject** of a sentence is the person or thing that **does the action**. The **verb** tells you what the action is.
  Ruby loves football.
  That house stands on a hill.
  Is your brother sleeping?

- The **object** of a sentence is the person or thing that the **action is done to**.
  The police officer caught the thief.
  Tom ate his dinner.
  I watched a play.

- Remember that in **passive** sentences, the **object** is the person or thing doing the action, and the **subject** is having the action done to it.
  The thief was caught by the police officer.

Pronoun subjects and objects

The **pronouns** we use depend on whether they are the **subject** or the **object** of the sentence.

I kissed her.

He helped me with Maths.

We heard them.

They beat us at Scrabble.

(green = subject pronoun; blue = object pronoun)

GET IT RIGHT!

- **Subjects** (green) and **objects** (blue) can be whole **phrases**, not just single **nouns** or **pronouns**.
  My next-door neighbour invited our whole family for tea.

- Remember that **more than one person or thing** can be the **subject** or **object** in the same sentence.
  Maya and Yasmin were driven to school by their mother and father.
  They owned two cats, three rabbits and a dog.

Sentences and clauses

You might be asked to identify **simple**, **compound** and **complex sentences**.

For example:

*Q: Rewrite the **two simple sentences** below to make **one compound sentence**.*

Max loves chips and chocolate.
Elsie likes healthy food.

Answer: *Max loves chips and chocolate but Elsie likes healthy food.*

Complex sentences

A **complex sentence** has a **main clause** and a **subordinate clause**.

Although I'm small, I'm very strong.

I'll give you my number if you give me yours.

When Sita arrived, she couldn't find her friends.

(green = main clause; blue = subordinate clause)

Relative clauses

A **relative clause** gives **extra information about** a **noun**. We often use **relative clauses** to say exactly **which** person or thing we are talking about. A **relative clause** usually **begins with** a **relative pronoun**.

I'm the girl <u>who</u> rescued your cat.

Are you the woman <u>whose</u> bag was stolen?

That's the hospital <u>where</u> my baby brother was born.

GET IT RIGHT!

- A **simple sentence** is made of just **one main clause**.
  I can ride a bike.

- A **compound sentence** has **two or more main clauses** joined together.
  *I can ride a bike **and** I can play chess.*

GET IT RIGHT!

- Remember that 'what' is **never used** as a **relative pronoun**.
  ✔ *the plants that/which grow in the greenhouse*
  ✗ *the plants what grow in the greenhouse*

- If the **noun** with the **relative clause** isn't the **subject** of the **clause**, you can leave out the **relative pronoun**.
  ✔ *the umbrella that I lost*
  ✔ *the umbrella I lost*

Conjunctions

You might be asked to use a **conjunction** in a sentence.

For example:

Q: *Complete the sentence with an appropriate* **subordinating conjunction**.

They went to the doctor's <u>because</u> William wasn't feeling well.

GET IT RIGHT!

- **Conjunctions** are words that **join** **phrases** or **clauses** in a sentence.
- When we join two **main clauses**, we use a **co-ordinating conjunction** such as 'and', 'or', 'but' or 'so'.
  Freddie swims lengths and Florence swims widths.
  They missed their plane so they will be late.
- When we join a **main clause** to a **subordinate clause**, we use a **subordinating conjunction** such as 'when', 'while', 'if', 'because' or 'although'.
  He loves weekends because he can sleep late.
- Remember that **subordinating conjunctions** can come at the beginning of a sentence. **If the** subordinate clause **comes first**, put a **comma** before the main **clause**.
  If we go shopping, let's take the car.

Connecting sentences and paragraphs

When we want to **connect sentences or** **paragraphs** to each other, we use **cohesive devices** such as 'however', 'therefore' or 'meanwhile'. We use them to show the relationship between ideas. They can be **single words or** **phrases**.

Zara wanted to make a cake. However, there was no flour in the cupboard. In addition, Dad had eaten all the chocolate! As a result, Zara had to go to the shops.

GET IT RIGHT!

- **Cohesive devices** usually come at the **beginning** of a sentence.
- Remember to write a **comma** after a **cohesive device**.

Verb tenses

You might be asked to use **verb tenses** correctly.

For example:

Q: *Complete the sentence below with the **simple past tense** of the **verbs** in brackets.*

My mother __was__ (to be) 18 when she __went__ (to go) to university and she __started__ (to start) work when she was 22.

GET IT RIGHT!

- We use the **simple present tense** for **things that happen now**.
  She dances in her bedroom.
  He loves his job.

- We use the **simple past tense** for **things that happened at a particular time in the past**. It is usually formed by adding 'd' or 'ed' to the **verb**.
  She danced in her bedroom.
  He loved his job.

- Remember that not all **verbs** follow the 'd' or 'ed' rule. You have to learn the exceptions!

take – took	*eat – ate*	*go – went*
have – had	*do – did*	*think – thought*
see – saw	*speak – spoke*	*catch – caught*

Present perfect

We use the **present perfect tense** for **things that happened in the past**, especially:

- with words like 'just', 'already', 'ever', 'never' and 'yet'
- when they affect the present in some way.

The **present perfect** is formed by using 'have' or 'has' and a **past tense verb**.

We have just arrived in France.

Abi has eaten too many sweets.

GET IT RIGHT!

- The past tense verb used in perfect tenses (e.g. *taken, eaten, gone, seen, spoken*) is **often different from the simple past tense** (took, ate, went, saw, spoke).
- 'has' and 'have' are often shortened to 's and 've (*We've arrived. Abi's eaten*).

Past perfect

We use the **past perfect tense** to talk about **things that happened before the events we are talking about now**. It is formed by using 'had' (often shortened to *'d*) and a **past tense verb**.

We had just arrived in France when the car broke down.

I'd given her my scarf because she was cold.

Present progressive

We use the **present progressive tense** to talk about **things that are happening right now**. It is formed by using the correct form of the **verb** 'be' followed by another **verb** ending with 'ing'.

Tarun is riding his bike.

My little sisters are climbing a tree.

Present progressive	Past progressive
are	was
is + ing	were + ing

Past progressive

We use the **past progressive tense** to talk about **things that were happening over a period of time in the past**. It is formed by using 'was' or 'were' followed by another **verb** ending with 'ing'.

I was crying all the way through the film.

We were trying not to laugh.

RATE YOUR PROGRESS!   'I can use verb tenses correctly.'

I'm fine ☐   Look again 🔍 ☐   Ask an adult ❓ ☐

Modal verbs

You might be asked to use **modal verbs** correctly.

For example:

Q: *Which sentence shows that you are most likely to play the piano tomorrow?*

a) *I could play the piano tomorrow.*

b) *I might play the piano tomorrow.*

c) *I shall play the piano tomorrow.*

d) *I should play the piano tomorrow.*

Answer: c) – 'I shall' means 'I will'.

Spelling modal verbs

You need to make sure you **spell modal verbs correctly**, especially the **contracted negative forms**.

shall	shan't
can	can't
could	couldn't
might	mightn't
must	mustn't
should	shouldn't
would	wouldn't

GET IT RIGHT!

- We use **modal verbs** with other **verbs**, e.g. to show whether something is **possible, likely, certain or necessary**.
  I shall send you a postcard.
  Jacob can't find his key.
  We mustn't make a noise.
  I think it might rain today.

- Remember that **modal verbs** can be used with other **tenses**.
  I could have done better.
  They wouldn't have come this way.

GET IT RIGHT!

- Remember to use 'have' and not 'of' when you use **modal verbs** in past **tenses**.
  ✗ *You should of left earlier.*
  ✔ *You should have left earlier.*

Active and passive

You might be asked to identify active and passive voices.

For example:

Q: *Which sentence is written in the **active voice**? Choose only* ***one*** *answer.*

a) *Spanish is spoken by millions of people.*

b) *My dad goes to work on a bike.* ✔

c) *The story was written by a famous author.*

d) *I was interviewed by a reporter.*

GET IT RIGHT!

- Sentences in the active voice **start with the people or things doing the action**.
  Our teacher conducts the school orchestra.
  England beat France last year.

- Sentences in the passive voice **start with the people or things having the action done to them**.
  The school orchestra is conducted by our teacher.
  France was beaten by England last year.

More about the passive voice

The passive voice is formed using the correct form of the verb 'be' and a past tense verb.

The window was broken.

In passive sentences, you don't always have to say who or what did the action.

That might be because **it doesn't matter**.

Your money will be returned.

It might be because **you don't know**.

My bike was stolen.

Or it might be because **you don't want to say!**

The sweets have been eaten.

GET IT RIGHT!

- Remember that in passive sentences, we use the preposition 'by' in front of the person or thing that does the action.
  The van was driven by the removal men.

RATE YOUR PROGRESS!   'I can identify active and passive voices.'
I'm fine ☐   Look again 🔍 ☐   Ask an adult ☐

41

Standard and non-standard English

You might be asked to identify **standard English**.

For example:

Q: *Which sentence is written in **standard English**? Choose only **one** answer.*

a) *She was going to the cinema.* ✔   c) *You could of helped me with my project.*

b) *We was stuck in a traffic jam.*   d) *Them pizzas look delicious.*

People speak in different ways, but remember to always write **standard English** in your school work.

✔ *I'm not going out.*   ✔ *You should have come.*

✘ *I ain't going out.*   ✘ *You should of come.*

Subject/verb agreement

The **subject** of a sentence must **agree** with the **verb**. That means that you need to use the correct form of the **verb**.

I was hungry.   We were hungry.   Safa has black boots.   The girls have black boots.
Remember that in **standard English**, you write:

✔ *we were*   ✘ *we was*   ✔ *they were*   ✘ *they was*

Them or those?

'Them' is a **pronoun**. It **replaces** a **noun**, so it **can never be used in front of a noun**.

✘ *Them ducks look hungry.*
✔ *Those ducks look hungry. I'm going to feed them.*

Double negatives

Words like 'haven't', 'no', 'don't', 'not' and 'never' are **negative** words. You should **only use one** of them **in a clause**.

✔ *We don't know any famous people.*   ✘ *We don't know no famous people.*

Past tense verbs

Some common **verbs** have different **irregular forms for different past tenses**. You need to know/learn which form to use.

✔ *I did my best.*   ✔ *I have done my best.*   ✘ *I done my best.*

✔ *I saw the movie.*   ✔ *I have seen the movie.*   ✘ *I seen the movie.*

42

Formal and informal language

You might be asked to identify **formal language**.

For example:

Q: *Which sentence is the most **formal**? Choose only **one** answer.*

a) *Phones are not permitted.*

b) *You won't use your phone, will you?*

c) *Leave your phone in your pocket!*

d) *I told you not to use that phone in the bathroom.*

Answer: a).

GET IT RIGHT!

- We use **informal language** with **friends and family**.
  The concert was totally awesome! We chatted to this guy in a really cool jacket.

- We use **formal** language for **serious writing**, e.g. in a letter to someone we don't know.
  The concert was extremely enjoyable.
  We spoke to a man in a very distinctive jacket.

Letter writing

You need the correct style of beginning and ending for letters.

	Beginning	Ending
Formal	Dear Ms Dubois,	Yours sincerely,
Formal	Dear Sir/Madam,	Yours faithfully,
Informal	Dear Mummy	Lots of love,
Informal	Dear Ravi	All the best,

GET IT RIGHT!

- Use 'Yours sincerely' **when you know the name** of the person you are writing to and 'Yours faithfully' **when you don't**.
- Use **expanded forms** (*do not; I will*) in **formal writing**, **not** contractions (*don't; I'll*).
- Remember to use **cohesive devices** in **formal writing** – you will get marks for using them correctly.

The subjunctive

The **subjunctive** is a **verb** form used in **formal writing** to talk about **things that should or could be done**, or for imaginary situations.

They insisted that we sit very still.

It is essential that he listen carefully.

If I were older, I'd learn to drive.

SATs practice: Sentence grammar and tenses

❶ Draw a line to match each sentence to its correct function. Use each function only once.

Sentence   **Function**

Listen to the teacher   Statement

Are you all listening   Command

What a lovely quiet classroom   Exclamation

Teachers like children who listen   Question

_____

1 mark

❷ Tick the option which shows how the underlined words in the sentence below are used.

Our friends arrived in <u>a big blue car with a sunroof</u>.

Tick **one**.

as a main clause   ⬜

as a noun phrase   ⬜

as a subordinate clause   ⬜   _____

as a relative clause   ⬜   1 mark

❸ Which sentence contains a **relative clause**?

Tick **one**.

We have lost all our matches this year.   ⬜

If you stay at my house, we can watch a film.   ⬜

You said that you were hungry.   ⬜   _____

The subject that I like best is Science.   ⬜   1 mark

4 Tick one box in each row to show if the sentence is in the **present progressive** or the **past progressive**.

Sentence	Present progressive	Past progressive
Laura was playing with her friends today.		
The girls are always running in the playground.		
Laura is getting more confident at school.		

1 mark

5 Rewrite the sentence below so that it is in the **active voice**. Remember to punctuate your sentence correctly.

The book was written by a famous author.

_____

_____

1 mark

Challenge yourself!

Was that all too easy? Challenge yourself with one final, tricky question!

6 Which verb completes the sentence so that it uses the **subjunctive form**?

If I _____ older, I would be able to go on the bus by myself.

Tick **one**.

be ☐   am ☐

was ☐   were ☐

1 mark

PART THREE: Punctuation

Sentence punctuation

You might be asked to use **capital letters** correctly.

For example:

Q: *Which sentence uses **capital letters** correctly?*

a) *I went on the train to London with my Friend Daniel.*

b) *i went on the train to London with my friend Daniel.*

c) *I went on the train to london with my friend Daniel.*

d) *I went on the train to London with my friend Daniel.* ✔

GET IT RIGHT!

- **Every sentence starts** with a **capital letter**.
  The train was very long. It went fast. Soon we were there.

- Remember that the word 'I' **always has a** **capital letter**, even in the middle of a sentence.
  I thought I knew the answer but I didn't.

- Always use a **capital letter** for **proper nouns**.
  Mr Morris gave us French homework on Thursday.

Punctuation at the end of a sentence

A **statement ends** with a **full stop**.

It has been windy today.

A **question ends** with a **question mark**.

When are you going on holiday?

An **exclamation ends** with an **exclamation mark**.

What a beautiful painting!

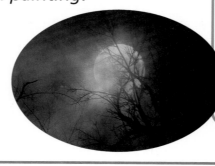

GET IT RIGHT!

- Remember that you **don't use** a **question mark** for **statements** like this:
  I wonder why he didn't come.
  Mum asked him if he needed help.

- An **ellipsis** is shown by **three dots** (…). You use it to show **pauses in speech**, or to show that **a sentence isn't finished**.
  'I hope you don't … er … think I'm … rude.'
  The moon came out from behind a cloud and suddenly …

RATE YOUR PROGRESS!   'I can use sentence punctuation correctly.'

I'm fine ▢   Look again 🔍 ▢   Ask an adult ▢

Commas

You might be asked to use **commas** correctly.

For example:

Q: *Insert a **pair of commas** in the correct place in the sentence below.*

Lucky Alfie, the best reader in the class, went home with a sticker from the teacher.

GET IT RIGHT!

- Writing a **comma** is like **making a** tiny **pause** when you are speaking.
- We often use **commas** in **complex sentences** when the **subordinate clause comes first**.
  <u>*When Jonny played football*</u>*, he wore red socks.*

- Extra information in sentences has **commas** around it.
  My best friend, who is called Sophie, has green eyes.
  Remember that the sentence should **still make sense** if you **take out the part inside the commas**.

Lists

You use **commas** to separate the items in a list. The commas go **between each item**.

I packed trousers, shirts, socks, shoes, pyjamas and a teddy bear.

You use commas for lists of **adjectives** and **verbs** too.

Nelly was small, clever, sporty, helpful and funny.

You can run, walk, jump, hop or crawl.

Remember that you **don't put a comma before 'and' or 'or' at the end** of a list.

Other places for commas

You use a **comma before a name** when you are talking to someone.

'Come on, Finn.'

You use a **comma after an adverbial phrase** at the beginning of a sentence (a **fronted adverbial**).

All night long, she lay awake worrying.

You usually use a **comma after a cohesive device**, **or before a conjunction**.

However, I decided not to stay.

He went to the shop, but didn't buy anything.

RATE YOUR PROGRESS!   'I can use commas correctly.'
  I'm fine ☀ 　 Look again 🔍 　 Ask an adult ❓ 　

47

Inverted commas/Speech marks

You might be asked to use **inverted commas** correctly.

For example:

Q: *Show where the missing **inverted commas** should go in the sentence below.*

'I hope you're listening to me,' said the teacher.

GET IT RIGHT!

- **Inverted commas** and **speech marks** are the same thing. We use them when we write speech, at the beginning and end of the speech. *'I've lost my purse,' said Mia.*

- You can write **inverted commas** like this: 'x' or like this: "x". Stick to the same style all through your writing.

Punctuation in speech

When the speech comes first, use a **comma**, **not** a **full stop**, **at the end** of the speech, even if it's a whole sentence.

'Your mum's going to be cross,' said Isaac.

When speech is a **question** or an **exclamation**, then use a **question mark** **(?)** or an **exclamation mark (!)**, not a **comma**.

When the speech comes after the other words, use a **comma in front of the inverted commas**.

Liam said, 'We'll help you find it.'

The speech always starts with a **capital letter**.

Use a **full stop**, **question mark** or **exclamation mark** at the end of the speech. This **punctuation always** goes **inside the inverted commas**.

Sonia shouted, 'I'll get the ball!'

'Where is it?' asked Josh.

GET IT RIGHT!

- **Direct speech** is the actual words that someone says. **Always use inverted commas** for **direct speech**. *'I've found my purse!' said Mia.*

- **Reported speech** is when we use our own words to say what someone said. **Never use inverted commas** for **reported speech**. *Mia said that she had found her purse.*

RATE YOUR PROGRESS!   *'I can use inverted commas/speech marks correctly.'*

I'm fine ☐   Look again 🔍 ☐   Ask an adult ❓ ☐

48

Brackets, dashes and hyphens

You might be asked to use **brackets**, **dashes** or **hyphens** correctly.

For example:

Q: *Insert a pair of* **brackets** *in the correct place in the sentence below.*

You need to bath dogs (especially poodles) if you want to keep their coats clean.

GET IT RIGHT!

- **Brackets** and **dashes** are used to **add extra information** to sentences. You put the **brackets** or **dashes** on either side of the extra information.
- **Brackets** look like this:
  The River Nile (which is in Egypt) is home to crocodiles.
- **Dashes** look like this:
  The River Nile – which is in Egypt – is home to crocodiles.
- **Leave a space between the dashes and the words** on either side.

Brackets and dashes at the end of sentences

If **brackets** are **at the end** of a sentence, the **second bracket** goes **before the last sentence punctuation**.

The Nile is home to crocodiles (animals with lots of sharp teeth).

If the information after a **dash** is **at the end** of the sentence, use a **single** dash.

The Nile is the world's longest river – it's in Egypt.

You can use a single **dash** to **indicate a pause,** or to **create drama**.

You won't believe what I saw – it was a helicopter!

I thought Leo was my friend – I was wrong!

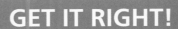

> The **formal name** for **brackets** is **parentheses**.

GET IT RIGHT!

- **Hyphens** are **shorter** than **dashes** and they do a different job.
- We use **hyphens** to **join words together** to make the meaning clearer.
  five-year-old girl; quick-thinking scientist; bad-tempered parrot

Colons

You might be asked to use **colons** correctly.

For example:

Q: *Insert a **colon** in the correct place in the sentence below.*

I bought all kinds of fruit: apples, bananas, grapes and pears.

GET IT RIGHT!

- We use a **colon** to **introduce a list**.
  These things are included in the price: flights, accommodation, coaches and evening meals.

- A **colon** comes **after** a **main clause**.

Bullet points

We often use a **colon** **before** a list of **bullet points**.

You will need the following ingredients:

- *225 grams of flour*
- *225 grams of sugar*
- *4 eggs*
- *225 grams of butter*
- *a spoonful of baking powder*

Bullet points are **clearer than long lists**, especially when the items on the list are **phrases** or **clauses**. You can put a **full stop** after each **bullet point** but you don't have to. Make sure they are all the same, though.

Colons in sentences

We use **colons** **between** **clauses** that are about the same topic, especially **to add more information**.

I wasn't hungry: I left a lot of food on my plate.

We also use **colons** **in front of** **phrases** to create a small pause **for dramatic effect**.

There's only one person I want when I'm feeling ill: my mother.

RATE YOUR PROGRESS! 'I can use colons correctly.'

I'm fine ☐   Look again 🔍 ☐   Ask an adult ? ☐

Semi-colons

You might be asked to use **semi-colons** correctly.

For example:

Q: *Insert **semi-colons** in the correct places in the sentence below.*

For lunch, I had two cheese sandwiches on brown bread; a little tub of pasta salad; a bar of my favourite chocolate; and a big juicy orange.

GET IT RIGHT!

- We use a **semi-colon between items in a list**, usually when the items are more than one word.
  At the shopping centre, we looked for a pair of new school shoes; a frying pan with a lid; a birthday present for Grandma; and some paper for the printer.

- Remember to **put a semi-colon before 'and' or 'or'** at the end of the list – this is different from **commas**, where you don't.

- When **semi-colons are not** in a list, don't use them too often. Just use one or two in one piece of writing.

Semi-colons in sentences

We use **semi-colons between main clauses** that are **about the same topic**, especially to show a contrast between two things.

Chloe went on holiday to Spain; Eva went to Scotland.

Some people get lots of work done in the morning; others work better late at night.

GET IT RIGHT!

- A **semi-colon** is a **bigger pause than** a **comma**, but **not as big as** a **full stop**.
- Remember that, **unlike** a **colon**, you **can't use a semi-colon before** a **phrase** or a single word. You must be able to divide a sentence with a **semi-colon** into two separate sentences.

RATE YOUR PROGRESS! | 'I can use semi-colons correctly.'

I'm fine ☀ ☐ Look again 🔍 ☐ Ask an adult ❓ ☐

Apostrophes

You might be asked to use **apostrophes** correctly.

For example:

Q: *Which sentence uses **apostrophes** correctly?*

a) *My sisters's friends had lunch together.*

b) *My sisters friend's had lunch together.*

c) *My sister's friends had lunch together.*

d) *My sisters friends' had lunch together.*

Answer: c) – my sister (singular) possesses friends, who don't possess anything here.

GET IT RIGHT!

- We use **apostrophes** **to show** who something belongs to. This is called **possession**.
- To show **possession for** a **singular** person or thing, you **add 's**.
  Toby's hopes of winning were high.
  The school's headteacher knows everyone.

- If the person's name ends in 's', you still **add 's.**
  I'm in Lucas's class.

- To show **possession for** **plural** words ending in 's', you just **add an apostrophe**, **without 's'**.
  The girls' houses were very close to each other.

Apostrophe problems

Apostrophes can be confusing. Here are two tips to help you get them right.

GET IT RIGHT!

- DON'T **use** an **apostrophe** **to make** a word **plural**.
  ✗ lots of *apple's*   ✗ lots of *banana's*
  ✔ lots of *apples*   ✔ lots of *bananas*

- DON'T **get confused between** 'its' and 'it's'.
  'its' is a **possessive pronoun** (*The dog scratched its ear*).
  'it's' is a **contracted form** of 'it is' or 'it has'
  (*It's easy to play the violin*).

Contractions

A **contraction**, also called a **contracted form**, is a word made by **joining two words together with** one or more **letters missed out**. The **apostrophe shows where the missing letters are**.

Original	Contraction
I am	I'm
he will	he'll
do not	don't
did not	didn't
cannot	can't
will not	won't
you are	you're
who is	who's

Here is the same sentence written in two different ways:

*I have given them directions so I do not know why they are not here yet. (*with **expanded forms***)*

*I've given them directions so I don't know why they aren't here yet. (*with **contracted forms***)*

GET IT RIGHT!

- The **contraction 's** can mean 'is' or 'has'.
  She's very clumsy. (= is)
  He's got brown hair. (= has)

- The **contraction 'd** can mean 'had' or 'would'.
  He'd lost his way. (= had)
  She'd always help people. (= would)

- Remember **not** to use **contractions** in formal **writing**.

RATE YOUR PROGRESS!   'I can use apostrophes correctly.'

I'm fine ☀ ▪   Look again 🔍 ▪   Ask an adult ❓ ▪

SATs practice: Punctuation

❶ Insert **full stops** and **capital letters** in the passage below so it is punctuated correctly.

My friend and i went to the seaside we made sandcastles on the beach and paddled in the sea then we had hot chocolate on the pier

_____

1 mark

❷ Which sentence is punctuated correctly?

Tick **one**.

I wondered what the noise was it was my – neighbour's radio! ⬭

I wondered – what the noise was it was my neighbour's radio! ⬭

I wondered what the noise was it was – my neighbour's radio! ⬭

I wondered what the noise was – it was my neighbour's radio! ⬭

_____

1 mark

❸ Which punctuation mark should be used in the place indicated by the arrow?

Lottie's favourite flowers are roses ↑ Grace prefers lilies.

Tick **one**.

comma ⬭

hyphen ⬭

semi-colon ⬭   _____

exclamation mark ⬭   1 mark

4 Insert **one comma** in the correct place in the sentence below.

Picking up her bag Auntie Angela strolled slowly to the gate.

_____

1 mark

5 Tick one box in each row to show whether the apostrophe is used for a **contracted form** or **possession**.

Sentence	Apostrophe for a contracted form	Apostrophe for possession
Give me George's book.		
Martha's dancing in her room.		
The koala's up a tree.		
Asha's hair has grown a lot.		

_____

1 mark

Challenge yourself!

Was that all too easy? Challenge yourself with one final, tricky question!

6 Which sentence uses the **colon** correctly?

Tick **one**.

We saw lots of animals: on the farm, sheep, horses, cows and chickens. ☐

We saw lots of animals on the farm: sheep, horses, cows and chickens. ☐

We saw: lots of animals on the farm, sheep, horses, cows and chickens. ☐

We saw lots of animals on the farm, sheep: horses, cows and chickens. ☐

_____

1 mark

Prefixes for meaning

> You might be asked to show you understand how **prefixes** affect meaning.

For example:

Q: *The **prefix** <u>re-</u> can be added to the word <u>create</u> to make the word <u>recreate</u>.*

*What does the word **<u>recreate</u>** mean?*

a) *to make stronger*

b) *to make wrong*

c) *to make too much*

d) *to make again*

Answer: d) – the prefix 're-' means 'again'.

GET IT RIGHT!

- A **prefix** is a group of letters that we **add to the start of a word**. It **changes the meaning** of that word.
- Some common **prefixes** are 'un-', 'over-' and 'under-'. *unhappy; overtired; undertake*

- The **basic word** that we add the **prefix** to is **called the** root word. *unhappy* (brown = prefix; blue = root word)

The prefix 'un-'

'Un-' is a very important **prefix**. You find it at the start of **adjectives**, **adverbs** and **verbs**. It means 'not' or 'the opposite of'.

un + kind = unkind

un + fortunately = unfortunately

un + pack = unpack

GET IT RIGHT!

- Remember that the spelling of the **root word stays the same** when the **prefix** is added.

Other important prefixes

There are many **prefixes**, all with different meanings. **Prefixes** are added to **adjectives**, **nouns** and **verbs**. These are some examples:

Prefix	Meaning	Examples
anti-	against	*antisocial; antibiotics*
auto-	(working) by itself	*automobile; automatic*
dis-	not	*to disapprove; to discontinue*
mis-	not or wrong	*misbehaviour; misfortune*
over-	too much	*overenthusiastic; to overact*

RATE YOUR PROGRESS! 'I can use prefixes correctly.'
I'm fine ☐   Look again 🔍 ☐   Ask an adult ❓ ☐

Suffixes for meaning

You might be asked to identify **suffixes**.

For example:

Q: *Circle the **two** words in this sentence that have **suffixes**.*

Electric light is very (powerful) but as soon as it goes out, you are left in (darkness).

Nouns made with suffixes

We can add 'ness' to make an **adjective** into a **noun**.

sad + ness = sadness

We can add 'ment' or 'er' to make a **verb** into a **noun**.

encourage + ment = encouragement

train + er = trainer

Adjectives made with suffixes

We can add 'ful' or 'less' to make a **noun** into an **adjective**.

care + ful = careful   *end + less = endless*

Verbs made with suffixes

We can add 'ise', 'ate' or 'ify' to make **nouns** or **adjectives** into **verbs**.

fossil + ise = fossilise   *hyphen + ate = hyphenate*

pure + ify = purify

Adverbs made with 'ly'

We can add 'ly' to make an **adjective** into an **adverb**.

quick + ly = quickly

selfish + ly = selfishly

painful + ly = painfully

Word families

You might be asked to give the meaning of a **root word** in a **word family**.

For example:

Q: *What does the root word* <u>astro</u> *or* <u>aster</u> *mean in the word family below?*

astronaut	**astro**nomer
asteroid	**astro**logy

a) *brave or strong*

b) *stars*

c) *oceans and seas*

d) *the future*

Answer: b).

GET IT RIGHT!

- A **word family** is a group of words that **all contain a part which is the same** (or very similar).
- The part that all the related words in a **word family** share is the **root word**, e.g. *friend, friendly, friendship*
  This is a **word family** and the **root word** is 'friend'.

Some important word families

There are a very large number of **word families** in English. The members of a **word family** are all linked in meaning even when they refer to very different things. Here are some examples of word families.

millimetre	**mill**ipede	**mill**igram	**mill**ennium

'mill' means 'a thousand'.

geo**graph**y	photo**graph**	auto**graph**	para**graph**

'graph' means 'writing' – it comes from Ancient Greek.

vision	in**vis**ible	tele**vis**ion	**vis**ibility

'vis' means 'see'.

pre**script**ion	film**script**	de**script**ion	manu**script**

'script' means 'writing' – it comes from Latin.

RATE YOUR PROGRESS! **'I can identify a root in a word family.'**

I'm fine ☀ ☐ Look again 🔍 ☐ Ask an adult ❓ ☐

Synonyms and antonyms

You might be asked to find a **synonym** or an **antonym**.

For example:

Q: *Choose a **synonym** for 'nervous'.*

a) *uneasy*   b) *silly*   c) *calm*   d) *fearless*

Answer: a).

GET IT RIGHT!

- **Synonyms** are words or **phrases** that have a **similar meaning** (*hot, warm, boiling, feverish*).
- Use **synonyms** to make your writing **more interesting** or **more precise**.
  Why use 'big' when you could use 'huge'?
  Why use 'huge' when you could use 'gigantic'?

Antonyms

Antonyms are words or **phrases** that have the **opposite meaning**. These pairs of words are all antonyms:

day – night   **bright** – dull   **tall** – short

cheap – expensive   **stop** – start   **love** – hate

More about synonyms and antonyms

When you choose a **synonym** or **antonym** to replace a word in a sentence, make sure that it is the **same type of word**.

Replace an adjective with another adjective.

Replace a noun with another noun.

GET IT RIGHT!

- Remember to choose **synonyms** and **antonyms** that are suitable for the sentence they are in.
  The worm wriggled across the grass.
  The worm crept across the grass.

- 'Wriggled' and 'crept' can be **synonyms**, but they aren't both suitable to describe a worm's movement!

RATE YOUR PROGRESS!   **'I can find synonyms and antonyms.'**

I'm fine ☀ ▢   Look again 🔍 ▢   Ask an adult ❓ ▢

SATs practice: Vocabulary

❶ Draw a line to match each word to the correct **suffix** to make an **adjective**.

Word

| hate |

| suit |

| poison |

Suffix

| able |

| ous |

| ful |

_____

1 mark

❷ Complete the passage with **adjectives** derived from the nouns in brackets. One has been done for you.

It was ___beautiful___ [beauty] up in the mountains.
We were so high that the scenery was really
_____ [drama]. We walked slowly because
the slippery path was _____ [danger].   _____

1 mark

Challenge yourself!

Was that all too easy? Challenge yourself with one final, tricky question!

3a Write an explanation of the word **synonym**.

_____

_____

3b Write one word that is a **synonym** of <u>surprised</u>.

_____

_____

2 marks

Spelling (Paper 2)

What's it all about?

Four things you need to know:

❶ The Key Stage 2 test paper for **Spelling** tests your **spelling skills**.

❷ The test lasts approximately **15 MINUTES** (but is not strictly timed).

❸ There will be **20 spellings** in total.

❹ The questions will all be the same type:

- each spelling will be presented in a sentence context, with the word to be spelt replaced by a line

- the sentences will be read aloud by a test administrator

- for each sentence, you will need to write the correctly spelt word on the line.

What skills are tested?

You will be tested on:

- **Plural forms** (regular and irregular plurals)

- **Prefixes for spelling** (including when to use double letters and hyphens)

- **Suffixes for spelling** (changing the root form)

- **Homophones** (too/to, there/their/they're, etc.)

- **Silent and unstressed letters** (examples of silent letters and unstressed vowels)

- **Confusing words** ('i' before 'e' rule and exceptions, double letters, 'ough' spellings, 'ch' spellings)

If all of this seems challenging, don't worry! There are pages on every one of these skills in the section that follows! So read on!

Plurals

You might be asked to spell a **plural** form.

For example:

It was dark outside, so we used ___torches___ .

GET IT RIGHT!

- A **plural** is **two or more** of something.
- To make most **nouns plural**, you just **add 's' to the end** of the word.
  car–cars   *plate–plates*   *zebra–zebras*
- If the word ends in the letters 's', 'x', 'z', 'sh' or 'ch', you **add 'es'**.
  kiss–kisses   *fox–foxes*   *church–churches*
- Some words have **irregular plurals** – see below.

Plurals with 'ies'

If a word ends in a **consonant** plus 'y', you make it **plural** by replacing the 'y' with 'i' + 'es'.

lorry – lorries   *factory – factories*   *spy – spies*   *mummy – mummies*

'o' words that need 'es'

Words that end in 'o' usually just have 's' at the end when they are **plural**. A few need 'es' on the end. You need to learn these.

potato – potatoes   *hero – heroes*   *echo – echoes*   *domino – dominoes*

Words ending in 'f' and 'fe'

To make a **plural** of a word that ends in 'f' or 'fe', you change the 'f' or 'fe' to 'v' and add 'es'.

life – lives   *shelf – shelves*   *wolf – wolves*   *thief – thieves*

A few **nouns** ending in 'f' do not follow this rule. To make them **plural**, you just put an 's' on the end. You need to learn these.

belief – beliefs   *chef – chefs*   *reef – reefs*   *roof – roofs*

Words with no plural

Some animal words stay the same in the plural.

one sheep – many sheep   *one deer – five deer*

one fish – hundreds of fish

RATE YOUR PROGRESS!   'I can spell plural forms.'

I'm fine ☼ ☐   Look again 🔍 ☐   Ask an adult ? ☐

Prefixes

You might be asked to spell a word with a **prefix**.

For example:

The patient was __unconscious__ so they called an ambulance.

GET IT RIGHT!

- Remember that a **prefix** is a group of letters, such as 'un-' or 'over-' that we **add to the start of a word**.
- A **prefix** **changes the meaning** of a word (*un + conscious = unconscious*).
- Adding a **prefix** **doesn't change the spelling** of the original word (the **root word**).

un + happy = unhappy	*over + tired = overtired*
dis + approve = disapprove	*re + place = replace*
mis + fortune = misfortune	*super + star = superstar*

Double letters

When a **prefix** **ends with the same letter** that the **root word** starts with, the new word contains **two letters together that are the same**. Sometimes this looks wrong, but it is correct.

mis + spell = misspell

un + necessary = unneccesary

im + mature = immature

ir + responsible = irresponsible

il + legible = illegible

over + rule + overrule

When a **prefix** **ends with** a **vowel** and the **root word** **starts with a vowel**, the new word has two **vowels** together. This can look strange, so people **sometimes put** a **hyphen** between the **prefix** and the **root word**.

co-ordinate instead of *coordinate*

re-enter instead of *reenter*

> Remember to be consistent. Always spell the same word with the same meaning in the same way.

Suffixes

You might be asked to spell a word with a **suffix**.

For example:

My mum loves making clothes, so she started a ___business___ .

GET IT RIGHT!

- Remember that a **suffix** is a group of letters, such as **'ness'** or **'ful'** that we **add to the end of a word**.
- A **suffix** **changes the meaning** of a word.
  busy (adjective) + *ness* = *business* (noun)
- Adding a **suffix** **often changes the spelling** of the original word (the **root word**).

Root words ending in 'e'

When the **root word** ends in 'e' and the **suffix** you're adding starts with a **vowel**, you drop the 'e'.

fortune + ate = fortunate   *juggle + er = juggler*

pure + ify = purify

Root words ending in a consonant plus 'y'

When the **root word** ends with a **consonant** plus 'y', the 'y' is replaced by an 'i'.

plenty + ful = plentiful   *angry + ly = angrily*

salty + ness = saltiness   *cheeky + ly = cheekily*

Adding the suffixes 'ed' and 'ing'

If a **verb** ends with one **vowel** plus a **consonant**, you double the **consonant** when you add the **suffixes** 'ing' or 'ed'.

clap – clapping – clapped

jog – jogging – jogged

stab – stabbing – stabbed

Remember that you add 'ing' or 'ed' to put a **verb** in a different **tense**.

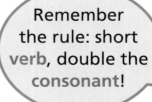

Remember the rule: short **verb**, double the **consonant**!

RATE YOUR PROGRESS!   'I can spell words with suffixes.'

I'm fine ☐   Look again 🔍 ☐   Ask an adult ❓ ☐

Homophones

You might be asked to spell a **homophone**.

For example:

It feels cold in here because there is a
___draught___ .

too/to

'To' is used to say where someone goes:

They drove to the supermarket.

'To' is also used to say why someone does something:

We left early to see the fireworks.

'Too' means 'more than you want':

You've given me too much pasta.

'Too' also means 'also':

Take me too!

Remember: 'Too' means 'more' or 'also'.

there/their/they're

'There' means 'that place':

Have you been there?

'Their' means 'belonging to them':

Their car is a lovely colour.

'They're' is short for 'they are':

They're following us.

than/then

To compare two things, use 'than':

Mo is cleverer than George.

For everything else, use 'then':

First, we'll have lunch and then we'll watch a movie.

hear/here

'Hear' is a **verb**. You hear the sounds that come through your ears:

Talk louder – I can't hear you!

'Here' means 'to/in this place':

You'll be safe here.

tail/tale

A 'tail' is part of an animal's body:

My dog wags his tail when I come home.

A 'tale' is a story:

A fairy tale usually has a happy ending.

accept/except

'Accept' means 'to agree to something':

We'd love to accept the invitation.

'Except' means 'but not':

They asked everyone except me.

RATE YOUR PROGRESS!   'I can spell homophones.'
I'm fine ☀ ☐   Look again 🔍 ☐   Ask an adult ❓ ☐

Silent and unstressed letters

You might be asked to spell a word with a silent letter.

For example:

Suddenly a ___knight___ on a white horse appeared.

GET IT RIGHT!

- **Silent letters** are letters that **can't be heard** when the word is spoken, like the 'k' in 'knight'.
- These words can be tricky to spell – **you need to learn them!**
- Below are some of the more common silent letters.

Silent 'g' and 'k' before the letter 'n'

campaign	foreign	gnome	reign
resign	knee	knife	knock

Silent 'h'

honest	ghost	rhyme	vehicle

Silent 'b' after 'm' or before 't'

debt	lamb	subtle	thumb

Silent 'w'

answer	two	whole	wriggle

Silent 't'

castle	fasten	listen	whistle

Some letters which are now silent used to be sounded hundreds of years ago!

Unstressed letters

Some words contain **vowels** that are **said clearly**, e.g. the 'a' in the word 'cat'. We call this a **'stressed'** vowel.

Other words contain **vowels** that are **not said clearly**. We call these **'unstressed'** vowels. A word may contain an unstressed 'a', 'e', 'i', 'o' or 'u' that sounds like 'uh', e.g. the first and last 'a' in 'banana'. In some words, you can't hear the unstressed vowel at all, e.g. the word 'different' sounds like it is spelt 'diffrent'.

Words with unstressed 'a'

hospital	separate	library

Words with unstressed 'e'

accident	general	offer

Words with unstressed 'i'

definite	family	medicine

Words with unstressed 'o'

doctor	factory	freedom

Confusing words and exceptions

You might be asked to spell a confusing word.

For example:

The spider crawled slowly across the ___ceiling___ .

GET IT RIGHT!

- The best known of all English spelling rules is **'i' before 'e' except after 'c'**.
- This rule helps you to remember the **order of** the **vowels 'i' and 'e' when they are together** in a word.
- For most words, you write 'i' and then 'e' (*piece, niece, believe*).
- Remember that if there's a 'c' before these **vowels**, you write 'e' then 'i' (*receive, deceive, ceiling*).

Exceptions to the rule

The 'i' before 'e' except after 'c' rule is only true when the sound made by 'ie' or 'ei' rhymes with 'tree'.

Words that **don't rhyme with 'tree' don't follow the rule**:

These words **do** have 'ie' after 'c':

ancient   science

These words have 'ei' but it's not after 'c':

their   height   weight

There are a few exceptions. Some words with 'ei' come after a letter that is not 'c', even though they **do** rhyme with 'tree'.

protein   seize

Double letters

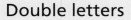

Double letters in words can be tricky. You need to learn these carefully. Some examples are:

cc	*according*	*occupy*	*success*
ff	*different*	*suffix*	*offer*
gg	*aggressive*	*struggle*	*beggar*
mm	*accommodate*	*communicate*	*immediately*
ss	*discussion*	*assist*	*possible*
pp	*equipped*	*apparent*	*opportunity*

Notice that all the words have short vowel sounds before the double letter, e.g. 'according' not 'ayccording'.

The different sounds of 'ough'

Lots of English words have the letters 'ough' in them. It's one of the trickiest spellings because it can be used to spell a number of different sounds. You have to **learn the different sounds for 'ough'**.

It can sound like 'stuff': *enough, rough, tough*

It can sound like 'off': *cough, trough*

It can sound like 'now': *plough, bough*

It can sound like 'port': *ought, nought, fought*

It can sound like 'other': *thorough, borough*

It can sound like 'roof': *through*

It can sound like 'slow': *although, dough*

Oh u greedy hippo!

The letters 'ch'

The letters 'ch' can be pronounced in different ways.

The most common sound is like 'ch' in 'cheese'.

chicken   *rich*   *chocolate*

Sometimes 'ch' sounds like the 'sh' in 'shape'.

chef   *chalet*   *machine*

Sometimes 'ch' sounds like the 'k' in 'king'.

scheme   *chemist*   *echo*

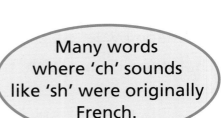

Many words where 'ch' sounds like 'sh' were originally French.

> ## GET IT RIGHT!
>
> - You need to **learn confusing spellings** so you get them right in the test!
> - **Learn the rules** first and **then learn the exceptions**.

SATs practice: Spelling

You will need to use the online audio file to help you with this SATs-style task. Find it at **yorknotes.com/primary/ks2/english/tests**.

Listen to each sentence and write down the correct spelling of the missing word.

❶ I was scared when I heard an _____ voice.

_____ 1 mark

❷ He had a _____ expression on his face.

_____ 1 mark

❸ It's important to make the _____ of your story exciting.

_____ 1 mark

❹ There's a sunflower _____ painted on the side of my uncle's van.

_____ 1 mark

❺ Imran is outside watching the _____ sunset.

_____ 1 mark

❻ We're hoping that our team will win the _____.

_____ 1 mark

❼ Some people believe in the _____ of aliens.

_____ 1 mark

❽ Rosie put down her knife and fork because she had eaten _____.

_____ 1 mark

❾ In bad weather, the farmer moves his _____ of cattle off the hillside.

_____ 1 mark

❿ David plays the trumpet in the school _____.

_____ 1 mark

York Notes SATs practice paper

How to approach your York Notes SATs practice paper

Work through these SATs practice papers calmly and carefully. Try to make the most of the time you have and complete as many questions as possible.

The Reading paper

- **Tackle** each text and set of questions in turn. Don't try to read all three texts in one go.

- **Read** the text and don't miss out parts. Try to spend 5–10 minutes reading it properly before you start answering questions.

- **Use** the information in the question to help you, e.g. it might tell you to look at a particular paragraph or phrase.

The Grammar, Punctuation and Spelling papers

- **Tackle** each question in turn, giving each one a go.

- **Read** the questions carefully to make sure you know what to do.

- **Use** the information you are given. In Paper 1, the **key words** in the question are always in **bold**.

Top tips!

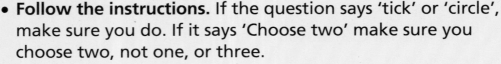

Try timing yourself! Complete each paper in the time allowed.

Give it your best shot!

- **Only answer what you have been asked.** Don't add anything extra – you won't get any marks for it!

- **Follow the instructions.** If the question says 'tick' or 'circle', make sure you do. If it says 'Choose two' make sure you choose two, not one, or three.

- **Look out for the marks.** If a question has two or three marks, you will need to do more than one thing!

- **Move on to the next question** if you are stuck. Come back to the tricky question later and have another go if you have time.

- **Read through your answers carefully** if you finish in time. This means reading each question again and making sure you have answered it correctly.

Don't worry if there seem to be lots of questions you don't know or are not sure about. Lots of other children will be feeling the same – and in any case, these papers are for practice. They will help you be as prepared as you can be!

Facing our fears

Ben looked down at his bowl of cornflakes with a frown. He couldn't eat them; he couldn't eat anything this morning. With a heavy heart, he put his bowl by the sink and went off in search of his shoes.

Silently, Mum handed Ben his shoes and watched patiently as he did up his laces – very, very slowly. She didn't say anything when he snagged his T-shirt in the zip of his coat, making a hole in it, and had to change into a new one. And she bit her tongue when he spent a full seven minutes looking for his gloves.

When Ben could think of no other way to procrastinate, they left the house and got into the car. As she drove, Mum hummed an old family favourite tune but Ben scowled and turned the radio on. This was the worst day of his life. His head hurt and he was sure he was getting a sore throat – it felt a bit scratchy – maybe if he was ill he wouldn't have to go …?

'You'll be fine, Ben, just as you were last time, and the time before that.' Mum smiled gently as they arrived. Ben opened the car door and looked up at the big green door with dread. He thought about his hero, astronaut Tim Peake, courageously opening the door of the space shuttle to spacewalk 250 miles above the Earth …

With nerves of steel, Ben pushed open the heavy door that read: *Dr Carlisle, DENTIST*.

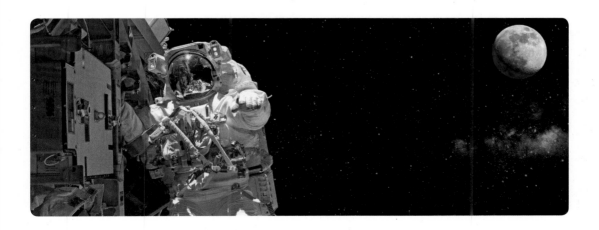

❶ Look at the first paragraph. Find and copy one phrase that suggests Ben is unhappy.

_____

_____

1 mark

❷ Why does Ben need to change his T-shirt?

_____

_____

1 mark

❸ Apart from his shoes, what two other items of outdoor clothing is Ben wearing as he leaves the house?

_____

_____

1 mark

❹ *And she bit her tongue when he spent a full seven minutes looking for his gloves.*

What does *bit her tongue* mean in this sentence? Tick one box.

became angry ☐

said nothing ☐

injured herself ☐

asked him to hurry ☐

_____

1 mark

❺ *When Ben could think of no other way to procrastinate, they left the house and got into the car.*

Choose the best word or phrase below to match the meaning of *procrastinate*. Tick one box.

repeat ⬭   delay ⬭   speed up ⬭   choose ⬭

_____

1 mark

❻ *This was the worst day of his life. His head hurt and he was sure he was getting a sore throat – it felt a bit scratchy – maybe if he was ill he wouldn't have to go …?*

Why does Ben start imagining he is ill?

_____

_____

1 mark

❼ Look at the paragraph beginning: *You'll be fine Ben, ….*

Find and copy a phrase which shows Ben is worried.

_____

_____

1 mark

❽ Look at the paragraph beginning: *You'll be fine Ben, ….*

Why does Ben think about his hero, Tim Peake, at this time? Give evidence from the text to support your answer.

_____

_____

_____

2 marks

9 *With nerves of steel, Ben pushed open the heavy door that read: Dr Carlisle, DENTIST.*

Look at the final paragraph. Find and copy a phrase that shows Ben is trying to be brave.

_____

_____

1 mark

10 The title of the story is 'Facing our fears'. What is Ben's fear in the story?

_____

_____

1 mark

11 In what ways does Mum try to make Ben feel better? List two ways, giving evidence from the text to support your answer.

_____

_____

_____

_____

_____

3 marks

SHARKS!

HAMMERHEAD SHARKS

Hammerhead sharks are one of the most remarkable types of sharks. There are ten different species of hammerheads, and they vary hugely in size and weight. The largest is the Great Hammerhead which is, on average, 3.5 metres long but can be up to 6 metres long and weigh 1,000 pounds. On the other hand, the smallest – the Bonnethead – is on average just under a metre long, which is about the size of a large dog.

It's easy to see why the hammerhead shark got its name! But its unique T-shaped head also serves a very useful purpose. The shark's eyes are very far apart and this helps with its vision. Hammerhead sharks have a visual field of 360° which means they can see around them at all times. This helps them find food.

And that is not their only means of sourcing food. All sharks have a sensory organ called an 'ampullae of Lorenzini', which allows them to detect electrical signals emitted by other living creatures in the water – even another animal's heartbeat! The hammerhead's ampullae is particularly sensitive. So they are even able to find stingrays that hide themselves in the sand at the bottom of the ocean!

Did you know?

1. The biggest shark is the Whale Shark. Its colossal body can be over 12 metres long. The smallest is the Dwarf Lantern Shark; it's only 15–20 centimetres long.

2. There are over 400 species of shark. Fewer than 7% of those species will attack a human.

3. There are on average 82 shark attacks each year worldwide.

4. New research shows that sharks might be colour-blind.

5. Some species of sharks lay eggs and some give birth to baby sharks called 'pups'.

75

An interview with Rob Evans: marine biologist

Rob, can you explain your job?

A marine biologist is someone who studies sea creatures. At the moment I'm working on a project that studies the impact of pollution on sharks.

How do you study the sharks?

Well, I literally put on my scuba diving equipment and get in the water! Fortunately I'm working in the Caribbean Sea at the moment so the water is lovely and warm. I observe the sharks (for as long as my oxygen tank will allow!) and take samples of the sea water.

And why do you need to study them?

Many species of sharks are endangered or what we call 'vulnerable'. That means their population is declining. It's upsetting to think about this, but I guess we have to face facts and try and deal with the issues.

What can we do to protect sharks?

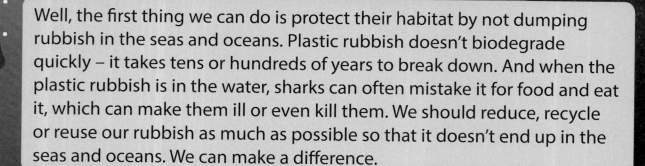

Well, the first thing we can do is protect their habitat by not dumping rubbish in the seas and oceans. Plastic rubbish doesn't biodegrade quickly – it takes tens or hundreds of years to break down. And when the plastic rubbish is in the water, sharks can often mistake it for food and eat it, which can make them ill or even kill them. We should reduce, recycle or reuse our rubbish as much as possible so that it doesn't end up in the seas and oceans. We can make a difference.

Do you enjoy your job?

It's the best job in the world!

❶ Which species of hammerhead shark can grow up to 6 metres long?

_____

_____

1 mark

❷ Explain why the hammerhead shark got its name, using evidence from the text.

_____

_____

1 mark

❸ Look at paragraphs 2 and 3. Give **two** ways the hammerhead sharks' bodies help them to find food.

_____

_____

_____

2 marks

❹ *All sharks have a sensory organ called an 'ampullae of Lorenzini', which allows them to detect electrical signals emitted by other living creatures in the water.*

What does the verb 'emit' mean in this sentence?

_____

_____

1 mark

❺ How do stingrays try to avoid hammerhead sharks?

_____

_____

1 mark

6 Look at the section headed: *Did you know?*

Its colossal body can be over 12 metres long.

What does 'colossal' mean in this sentence?

_____

1 mark

7 There aren't many species of shark that will attack a human.
Find and copy evidence from the text to show this.

_____

1 mark

8 Put these sharks in order of size. Number the boxes 1–4 with
1 being the largest and 4 the smallest.

Great Hammerhead ⬜

Dwarf Lantern Shark ⬜

Whale Shark ⬜

Bonnethead ⬜

1 mark

9 Look at the interview with Rob Evans. Using information from
the interview, tick one box in each row to show whether each
statement is a **fact** or an **opinion**.

	Fact	Opinion
The Caribbean Sea is warm.		
Many species of shark are endangered.		
Being a marine biologist is the best job in the world.		

1 mark

10 Look at Rob's answer to the question: *What can we do to protect sharks?* Give **two** things he says humans could do.

_____

_____

_____

2 marks

11 Rob seems very fond of sharks. Find **three** pieces of evidence in the interview that supports this.

_____

_____

_____

_____

3 marks

12 Draw lines to match each description of the text type with the correct text title.

A personal account of working with sharks	*Hammerhead sharks*
Some fun and interesting facts about sharks	*Did you know?*
A factual description of how certain sharks are able to find food	*An interview with Rob Evans*

_____

1 mark

Reading Paper Text 3: Fiction

Message in a bottle

Lia and Jack stepped inside the huge mouth of the cave. The summer sun provided shafts of illumination, although there were dark, gloomy shadows at the back of the cavernous hollow.

Taking their trainers off, they walked barefoot over the golden sand, which crunched like biscuits with each step. A trickle of water snaked along beside them and they saw it led to a pool which shimmered invitingly in the golden light. Soon they'd plunged in, and were gleefully splashing around happily oblivious to everything else.

'Our own private swimming pool!' shouted Jack with excitement, his words reverberating around the dome of the cave, before disappearing into the nooks and crannies. Eventually, they pulled themselves out and dried off.

'Jack – look at that! What is it?' Lia gasped as a ray of sunlight bounced off a piece of green glass twinkling at the back of the cave. 'It's glass – I think it's a bottle. And it looks like there's a piece of paper rolled up inside the neck. And a cork in the top – can you see it?'

'It's half buried, it's hard to tell,' said Jack. He shivered suddenly. 'I'm cold – come on, let's go!'

He was right – it was cold. The sun had dipped and Lia knew they ought to be going.

Jack turned to go, and suddenly halted. 'Look!' he shouted to Lia. She turned away from the bottle and followed his gaze. The little stream was now a torrent of frothing grey water, devouring the sand and pebbles.

'It's the tide,' said Lia, her heart thudding like a drum. 'We should have checked first! There's no way we can go back.' She stared up at the imposing rock face glaring down at them sternly. 'There's a chink of light – between those two slabs of stone. That must be our way out…'.

They slid between the two columns of stone, and then pulled themselves up onto a damp, mossy ledge. Above them they could see an envelope of sunlight but to get to it would mean slithering on their bellies like lizards through a low tunnel.

'I'm not sure I can do this,' said Jack, doubtfully, gazing at the narrow gap through which they'd have to crawl. 'I think I'd rather swim for it.'

'Don't be daft. This is the only exit,' said Lia. She dropped onto her haunches, then onto her front and began to worm her way through the tunnel. Jack sighed, and did the same.

After half an hour of struggle, sweat and dirt – and quite a few scratches and bruises – they hauled themselves through the tiny space and collapsed onto the grassy clifftop. Gasping for breath, they stared up at the wispy clouds turning orange and pink as the sunset spread across the sky.

Eventually, Lia spoke. 'I wonder what was written on that piece of paper.'

'Oh no,' said Jack. He knew Lia too well, and didn't like the flicker of curiosity in her eye. 'We're not doing it, not even when the tide is out.'

❶ *Taking their trainers off, they walked barefoot over the golden sand, which crunched like biscuits with each step.*

Choose the best word(s) to match the description above. Circle your choice.

The sand is: crispy   wet and soft   hard and rippled

_____

1 mark

❷ Look at the first three paragraphs. Tick one box in each row to show whether the statement is **true** or **false**.

	True	False
The cave has a big entrance.		
The pool looks a bit scary.		
The children enjoy being in the pool.		
They spend a short time in the pool.		

_____

1 mark

❸ Look at the paragraph beginning: *Jack – look at that! What is it?* Give **three** details from the text about the bottle Lia sees.

_____

_____

_____

_____

2 marks

4 *He shivered suddenly. 'I'm cold – come on, let's go!'*
He was right - it was cold. The sun had dipped and Lia knew
they ought to be going.

How has the mood changed from the beginning of the story?
Give evidence from the text to support your answer.

_____

_____

         _____

2 marks

5 How does the small stream of water in the cave change?

_____

         _____

1 mark

6 Look at the paragraph beginning: *'It's the tide,' said Lia.*

Find and copy one word that means to make a
strong impression.

_____

         _____

1 mark

7 *… slithering on their bellies like lizards through a low tunnel.*

This describes how the children **think** they will have to move
through the tunnel. Find and copy another phrase that
describes how they **do** move through the tunnel.

_____

         _____

1 mark

8 Lia tells Jack how they can escape from the cave.

How does Jack feel about her plan? Explain your answer with evidence from the text.

_____

_____

_____

_____

_____

3 marks

9 What part of the day is it when they finally emerge from the cave?

_____

_____

1 mark

10 Look at the paragraph beginning: *After half an hour of struggle ....*

Why do the children stare up at the sky?

_____

_____

1 mark

⑪ Number the following events 1–5 to show the order in which they happened.

The first one has been done for you.

Jack notices that the tide is coming in. ⬜

The children climb out of the cave. ⬜

Lia notices light coming through a hole at the top of the cave. ⬜

The children enter the cave. ①

Lia spots a glass bottle at the back of the cave. ⬜

_____

1 mark

⑫ *'Oh no,' said Jack. He knew Lia too well, and didn't like the flicker of curiosity in her eye. 'We're not doing it, not even when the tide is out.'*

Predict what will happen next in the story. Use evidence from the text to support your prediction.

_____

_____

_____

_____

_____

2 marks

Grammar, punctuation and vocabulary test (Paper 1)

❶ Circle all the **nouns** in the sentence below.

I like the pictures of kings and queens best of all.

_____ 1 mark

❷ Tick the sentence that must end with a **question mark**.

	Tick **one.**
How you found him isn't the point	◯
When the alarm goes off, everyone must leave	◯
Why do some people find Maths difficult	◯
What they're doing is really unfair	◯

_____ 1 mark

❸ Complete each sentence by writing the missing **determiner**.

There may be more than one correct answer.

This morning, _____ sun is shining.

Let's go for _____ picnic.

Later, we'll have _____ ice cream.

_____ 1 mark

❹ Insert **commas** in the sentence below so it is punctuated correctly.

Adam went to the post office the bakery the bank and the petrol station.

_____ 1 mark

❺ Complete the sentence below by writing the **conjunctions** from the box in the correct places. Use each conjunction only **once**.

but   or   and

You can go into the classroom _____ sit at your tables, _____ if I see anyone running _____ shouting, you will all come out again.

_____ 1 mark

❻ Replace the underlined word or words in the sentence below with the correct **pronouns**.

Sarah went to the circus with her friends and _____ (her friends) gave _____ (Sarah) a lift.

_____ 1 mark

❼ Draw a line to match each sentence to its correct **function**. Use each function box only **once**.

Sentence   Function

How healthy your dinner is   statement

Eat your salad   question

Vegetables are good for you   exclamation

You like cabbage, don't you   command

_____ 1 mark

❽ Circle the **two** words that show the **tense** in the sentence below.

He wore boots and a warm coat – there was snow on the ground.   _____ 1 mark

9 Insert a **pair of commas** in the correct places in the sentence below.

Mr Sullivan our next-door neighbour bought my dad's old bike.

_____ 1 mark

10 Which sentence uses **capital letters** correctly?

Tick **one**.

The Teacher at my old School was very kind. ☐

My brother has gone on a School Trip today. ☐

We went to London on a red Bus. ☐

Have you seen the new James Bond film? ☐

_____ 1 mark

11 Insert a **semi-colon** in the correct place in the sentence below.

I sing and play the trumpet I love all kinds of music.

_____ 1 mark

12 Tick **one** box in each row to show whether the underlined clause is a **main clause** or a **subordinate clause**.

Sentence	Main clause	Subordinate clause
<u>Give me a shout</u> when you've finished.		
<u>If you read the notes</u>, it's easy to play the recorder.		
I wore my green wellies <u>because it was raining.</u>		

_____ 1 mark

13 Which sentence is punctuated correctly?

Tick **one**.

You can find out more later see page (25). ☐

You can find out more later (see page 25.) ☐

You can find out more later (see page 25). ☐

You can find out more later see (page 25). ☐

_____ 1 mark

14 Which sentence is an **exclamation**?

Tick **one**.

What are you making for lunch ☐

What a delicious lunch this is ☐

I asked you to make some lunch for me ☐

Sit down and eat lunch with me ☐

_____ 1 mark

15 Which sentence uses the word <u>match</u> as a **verb**?

Tick **one**.

It is not safe to strike a <u>match</u> in here. ☐

We saw an exciting <u>match</u> yesterday. ☐

Dark chocolate is the perfect <u>match</u> for ripe strawberries. ☐

His trousers don't <u>match</u> his shirt. ☐

_____ 1 mark

16 Insert a **pair of dashes** in the correct places in the sentence below.

The tall plant the one in the hall needs watering.

_____ 1 mark

17 Circle the **two adverbs** in the sentence below.

She slammed the door violently because she was so angry.

_____ 1 mark

18 Which sentence is punctuated correctly?

Tick **one**.

The doctor said 'I hope you feel better soon' ☐

The doctor said, 'I hope you feel better soon.' ☐

The doctor said, 'I hope you feel better soon' ☐

The doctor said, 'I hope you feel better soon'. ☐

_____ 1 mark

19 Which sentence uses the **present perfect form**?

Tick **one**.

On Friday, I took my hamster to the vet. ☐

They are waiting for you by the bus stop. ☐

We have had such a lovely day today. ☐

Marianne was having a birthday party. ☐

_____ 1 mark

20 Insert **full stops** and **capital letters** in the passage below so it is punctuated correctly.

Penguins live in the Antarctic where it is very cold they lay their eggs on the ice and they swim in the freezing water they are amazing animals

_____ 1 mark

21 Circle the word in the passage that contains an **apostrophe for possession**.

I'm sorry about yesterday – I hope you weren't upset.
My sister's friend came to visit so I couldn't see you.

_____ 1 mark

22 Which **verb form** completes the sentence?

As soon as Julia _____ her homework, she turned on the television.

Tick **one**.

is finishing ☐

had finished ☐

was finishing ☐

has finished ☐   _____ 1 mark

23 Which sentence is the most **formal**?

Tick **one**.

You will reply quickly, won't you? ☐

Please reply within a week. ☐

Get back to me by the end of the week! ☐

It is essential that you reply within one week. ☐   _____ 1 mark

24 Rewrite the verbs in the boxes to complete the sentences with the correct choice of **tense**.

After they _____, they left the restaurant.   to eat

I always _____ the door when I go out.   to lock

_____ 1 mark

25 Circle the **conjunction** in each sentence.

If we're late, we'll miss the beginning of the film.

When I visit my grandparents, they always let me stay up late.

The adults cooked lunch while the children played in the garden.

_____ 1 mark

26 Circle all the **prepositions** in the sentence below.

Please leave your books on the table, make a line by the door and walk slowly to the hall.

_____ 1 mark

27 Rewrite the underlined verbs in the sentences below so that they are in the **past progressive** form.

The children _____ (bake) a cake. They _____ (mix) the ingredients in a bowl.

_____ 1 mark

28 Label each of the **clauses** in the sentence below as either **main (M)** or **subordinate (S)**.

The children were frightened but when they heard the scream, they crept into the cave.

_____ 1 mark

29 Circle the **relative clause** in the sentence below.

The lady who lives next door is a singing teacher.

_____ 1 mark

30 The **prefix** <u>over-</u> can be added to the word <u>tired</u> to make the word <u>overtired</u>.

What does the word **overtired** mean?

Tick **one.**

very tired   ◯

not tired   ◯

too tired   ◯

a bit tired   ◯   _____ 1 mark

31 Circle the **possessive pronoun** in the passage below.

Are you sure that cardigan belongs to you?
It looks the same as mine. Please look in the
drawer and see if your cardigan is there.   _____ 1 mark

32 Circle the **two** words that are **antonyms** in the sentence below.

Despite the sea's calm appearance, the surfers were afraid
that the waves would be rough later in the day.

_____ 1 mark

33 a) Write a **command** which could be the first step in instructions
     for crossing the road.

Remember to punctuate your answer correctly.

_____

b) Write a **question** as a heading for instructions for crossing the
     road. Remember to punctuate your answer correctly.

_____

_____

_____ 2 marks

34 Insert a **pair of brackets** in the correct place in the sentence below.

My friend Katie is 5 feet 6 inches over 1.5 metres tall.

_____ 1 mark

35 What does the root word <u>audi</u> mean in the **word family** below?

audible   **audi**ence   **audi**torium   **audi**obook

Tick **one**.

quiet   ☐

in a group   ☐

music   ☐

hearing   ☐

_____ 1 mark

36 a) Circle the **object** in the sentence below.

At the weekend, I washed the dog.

b) Circle the **subject** in the sentence below.

In London, Josie went to the Science Museum with Uncle Ed.

_____ 2 marks

37 Rewrite the sentence below as **direct speech**. Remember to punctuate your answer correctly.

Oliver asked me if I was feeling tired.

Oliver asked me, _____

_____ 1 mark

38 Which sentence shows that you are **most likely** to play football?

Tick **one**.

I shall play football. ◯

I might play football. ◯

I should play football. ◯

I could play football. ◯

_____ 1 mark

39 Circle the **relative pronoun** in the sentence below.

I put on my swimming costume and dived into your swimming pool which was fairly deep.

_____ 1 mark

40 Which sentence uses the **hyphen** correctly?

Tick **one**.

That fair haired-girl is my cousin Meg. ◯

That fair haired girl is my cousin-Meg. ◯

That fair-haired-girl is my cousin Meg. ◯

That fair-haired girl is my cousin Meg. ◯

_____ 1 mark

41 Complete the sentence below with the **simple past tense** of the underlined verbs. One has been done for you.

We ___ordered___ (to order) our food, but I _____ (to think)

the menu _____ (to be) very confusing.

_____ 1 mark

42 **a)** Write an explanation of the word **synonym**.

_____

_____

b) Write **one** word that is a **synonym** of <u>know</u>.

_____

_____ 2 marks

43 Rewrite the sentence below as **direct speech**.

Remember to punctuate your answer correctly.

He said she could go without him.

He said, _____

_____ 1 mark

44 Write a **noun phrase** containing at least **three** words to complete the sentence below.

My favourite animals are _____.

_____ 2 marks

45 **a)** Rewrite the sentence below so that it is in the **active voice**. Remember to punctuate your sentence correctly.

Our car was mended by the mechanic.

_____

b) Rewrite the sentence below so that it is in the **passive voice**. Remember to punctuate your sentence correctly.

Many people speak Spanish.

_____

_____ 2 marks

46 Complete the sentence below so that it uses the **subjunctive form**.

If I _____ to live in another country, I would choose Italy.

_____ 1 mark

Spelling test (Paper 2)

You will need to use the online audio file to help you with this SATs-style task. Find it at **yorknotes.com/primary/ks2/english/tests**.

Listen to each sentence and write down the correct spelling of the missing word.

❶ The fridge was _____ empty this morning.

_____ 1 mark

❷ There is no need to _____ the party.

_____ 1 mark

❸ Most clothes are made by _____ in factories.

_____ 1 mark

❹ If you go out to eat every day, it's not a _____ treat.

_____ 1 mark

❺ Lara _____ a confusing email from her teacher.

_____ 1 mark

❻ We have a _____ staying for the weekend.

_____ 1 mark

❼ My grandparents love _____ in all seasons.

_____ 1 mark

❽ Our school had a visit from a _____ football player.

_____ 1 mark

❾ Licking ice cream with your _____ makes it last longer.

_____ 1 mark

❿ Samuel will do well because he has plenty of _____.

_____ 1 mark

⑪ _____ I have no pets, I am an animal lover.

_____ 1 mark

⑫ The detectives could not solve the _____.

_____ 1 mark

⑬ Lettie thinks her bedroom is tidy but her mother _____.

_____ 1 mark

⑭ When we study _____, we understand our planet better.

_____ 1 mark

⑮ My cat's favourite _____ is sleeping in front of the oven.

_____ 1 mark

⑯ The play was too long so the director cut some _____.

_____ 1 mark

⑰ You have gone to a lot of _____ to make lunch.

_____ 1 mark

⑱ Our _____ has lived in the street for fifty years.

_____ 1 mark

⑲ The box was _____ lighter than I expected.

_____ 1 mark

⑳ There is no _____ at all in my mind.

_____ 1 mark

Answers

Section One: Reading Paper

SATs practice

1. **1 mark**

   funny

2. **1 mark**

   oars

3. **1 mark**

   Any example of alliteration is acceptable (e.g. each **b**ird a **b**oat / **w**ide **w**aterway / **s**tealthily **s**uck)

4. **1 mark**

   weasel

   fox

   rats

5. **1 mark**

   Because of the danger from weasels and foxes

6. **1 mark**

   2

   4

   3

   1

7. **2 marks** (1 mark for each adjective)

   Evidence: He uses adjectives such as 'beautiful' and 'comical'.

Section Two: Grammar, punctuation and vocabulary

Part One: Word types/classes

Nouns

The **girls** were eating **toast** in the **kitchen**.

Pronouns

When Joe got home, **he** was hungry.

Joe went to the fridge and opened **it**.

Determiners

I saw **an** alligator in **a** pond when I went to **the** zoo.

Verbs

Can you **touch** your toes?

Adjectives

I used my **right** hand.

Adverbs

Harry walked **quickly** because he was late for school.

Prepositions

Dad stayed **at** home but I went **to** the park **with** Mum.

1. adverb

2. When we arrived at the hotel, Mum told us which room was **ours**. The bed by the window was **mine** and my sister had the bed by the door.

3. Charlie is sitting behind his friend.

   I'll be there at six tomorrow.

4. Have you seen the book **that** I was reading?

5. I've got **a** new baby sister.

   I used to be **an** only child.

   Being a big brother is **the** best thing.

6. I'll cover the table with a pretty cloth.

Part Two: Sentence grammar and tenses

Sentence functions

What food do cats like best?

Clauses

She did well in the competition, despite feeling tired.

If you don't need it, **give it to a charity shop.**

Although they loved dogs, **they chose a cat.**

Phrases

The boys walked **very slowly**.

Subject and object

Next week, I am taking **Jack** to the seaside.

Simple, compound and complex sentences

Max loves chips and chocolate, but Elsie likes healthy food.

Conjunctions

because

Verb tenses

was

went

started

Modal verbs

I shall play the piano tomorrow.

Active and passive

My dad goes to work on a bike.

Standard and non-standard English

She was going to the cinema.

Formal and informal language

Phones are not permitted.

SATs practice

1. Listen to the teacher → command

   Are you all listening → question

   What a lovely quiet classroom → exclamation

   Teachers like children who listen → statement

2. as a noun phrase

3. The subject that I like best is Science.

4

Sentence	Present progressive	Past progressive
Laura was playing with her friends today.		✔
The girls are always running in the playground.	✔	
Laura is getting more confident at school.	✔	

5. A famous author wrote the book.

6. If I **were** older, I would be able to go on the bus by myself.

Part Three: Punctuation

Sentence punctuation

I went on the train to London with my friend Daniel.

Commas

Lucky Alfie, the best reader in the class, went home with a sticker from the teacher.

Inverted commas/speech marks

'I hope you're listening to me,' said the teacher.

Brackets, dashes and hyphens

You need to bath dogs (especially poodles) if you want to keep their coats clean.

Colons

I bought all kinds of fruit: apples, bananas, grapes and pears.

Semi-colons

For lunch, I had two cheese sandwiches on brown bread; a little tub of pasta salad; a bar of my favourite chocolate; and a big juicy orange.

Apostrophes

My sister's friends had lunch together.

SATs practice

1. My friend and **I** went to the seaside. **W**e made sandcastles on the beach and paddled in the sea. **T**hen we had hot chocolate on the pier.

2. I wondered what the noise was – it was my neighbour's radio!

3. Lottie's favourite flowers are roses; Grace prefers lilies.

4. Picking up her bag, Auntie Angela strolled slowly to the gate.

5.

Sentence	Apostrophe for a contracted form	Apostrophe for possession
Give me George's book.		✔
Martha's dancing in her room.	✔	
The koala's up a tree.	✔	
Asha's hair has grown a lot.		✔

6. We saw lots of animals on the farm: sheep, horses, cows and chickens.

Prefixes for meaning

to make again

Suffixes for meaning

Electric light is very **powerful** but as soon as it goes out, you are left in **darkness**.

Word families

stars

Synonyms and antonyms

uneasy

SATs practice

1. hate**ful**

   suit**able**

   poison**ous**

2. beautiful

   dramatic

   dangerous

3. Suggested answers:

   a) A synonym is a word that has the same meaning as another word.

   b) Suggested answers:

      amazed

      astonished

      shocked

Section Three: Spelling

SATs practice

1. I was scared when I heard an **unfamiliar** voice.

2. He had a **solemn** expression on his face.

3. It's important to make the **beginning** of your story exciting.

4. There's a sunflower **symbol** painted on the side of my uncle's van.

5. Imran is outside watching the **incredible** sunset.

6. We're hoping that our team will win the **competition**.

7. Some people believe in the **existence** of aliens.

8. Rosie put down her knife and fork because she had eaten **enough**.

9. In bad weather, the farmer moves his **herd** of cattle off the hillside.

10. David plays the trumpet in the school **orchestra**.

Section Four: SATs Practice Papers

Facing our fears

1. **1 mark**

   With a heavy heart… / …with a frown

2. **1 mark**

   Because he snagged / caught his T-shirt in the zip of his coat and made a hole in it

3. **1 mark**

   A coat and some gloves

4. **1 mark**

   said nothing

5. **1 mark**

   Ben was trying to **delay** leaving the house.

6. **1 mark**

   So that he doesn't have to go to the dentist's

7. **1 mark**

   'with dread'

8. Up to **2 marks**

   Point: Because he thinks Tim Peake is brave, and he wants to be brave. (**1 mark**)

   Evidence: 'He thought about his hero, astronaut Tim Peake, courageously opening the door...' (**1 mark**)

9. **1 mark**

   'With nerves of steel'

10. **1 mark**

    He's facing his fear of dentists / going to the dentist's.

11. Up to **3 marks**

    3 marks for both points, supported with evidence from the text

    2 marks for both points, with one supported by evidence from the text

    1 mark for both points, with no supporting evidence from the text

    Point: Ben's mum is patient with Ben. Evidence: She helps him find his shoes and she doesn't hurry him when he spends a long time looking for his gloves.

    Point: Mum is kind. Evidence: She hums an old family favourite tune to comfort him and reassures him that he'll be fine.

Sharks!

1. **1 mark**

   Great Hammerhead

2. **1 mark**

   because of its 'unique T-shaped head'

3. Up to **2 marks**

   They have 360° vision due to their eyes being far apart, so they can find their food. (**1 mark**)

   They have a very sensitive ampullae which means they can easily find other animals by their electrical signals. (**1 mark**)

4. **1 mark**

   to send out something

5. **1 mark**

   They bury themselves in the sand at the bottom of the ocean.

6. **1 mark**

   very big

7. **1 mark**

   Fewer than 7% of those species will attack a human.

8. **1 mark**

Great Hammerhead	2
Dwarf Lantern Shark	4
Whale Shark	1
Bonnethead	3

9. **1 mark**

	Fact	Opinion
The Caribbean Sea is warm.	✔	
Many species of shark are endangered.	✔	
Being a marine biologist is the best job in the world.		✔

10. Up to **2 marks**

We should protect their habitat by not dumping rubbish in the seas and oceans. (**1 mark**)

We should reduce, reuse and recycle our rubbish so it doesn't end up in the seas and oceans. (**1 mark**)

11. Up to **3 marks (**1 mark for each piece of evidence)

1. He observes sharks for as long as he can: 'for as long as my oxygen tank will allow'.

2. He says his job is 'the best in the world'.

3. He finds it upsetting that 'their population is declining'.

12. **1 mark**

A personal account of working with sharks: An interview with Rob Evans

Some fun and interesting facts about sharks: Did you know?

A factual description of how certain sharks are able to find food: Hammerhead sharks

Message in a bottle

1. **1 mark**

The sand is **crispy**.

2. **1 mark**

	True	False
The cave has a big entrance.	✔	
The pool looks a bit scary.		✔
The children enjoy being in the pool.	✔	
They spend a short time in the pool.		✔

3. Up to **2 marks** (1 mark for a correct detail, 1 mark for all 3 correct details)

it's green

there's a piece of paper rolled up inside the neck

there's a cork in the top

4. Up to **2 marks**

Point: The atmosphere changes from happy and fun (positive) to negative. (**1 mark**)

Evidence: The writer used lots of positive language in the beginning of the story (e.g. the summer sun provided shafts of illumination, shimmered invitingly, golden sand, splashing around happily, twinkling, shouted Jack with excitement) and then the language becomes more negative (e.g. shivered, cold, the sun had dipped, ought to). (**1 mark**)

5. **1 mark**

It is now a torrent of grey frothing water.

6. **1 mark**

'imposing'

7. **1 mark**

   Lia 'began to worm her way through the tunnel'.

8. Up to **3 marks** (1 mark for the point; 2 marks for the point plus one piece of evidence; 3 marks for the point plus two pieces of evidence)

   Point: Jack is reluctant to follow Lia's plan. (**1 mark**)

   Evidence:

   'I'm not sure I can do this,' said Jack, doubtfully …

   'I think I'd rather swim for it.'

   Jack sighed, and did the same.

9. **1 mark**

   early evening / dusk

10. **1 mark**

    because they are lying on their backs after all the exertion of the climb (or possibly because they were glad to see the open expanse of the sky after feeling trapped in a dark cave)

11. **1 mark**

Jack notices that the tide is coming in.	③
The children climb out of the cave.	⑤
Lia notices light coming through a hole at the top of the cave.	④
The children enter the cave.	①
Lia spots a glass bottle at the back of the cave.	②

12. Up to **2 marks**

    Prediction: Lia will go back into the cave to find the message in the bottle. (**1 mark**)

Evidence: Jack sees a 'flicker of curiosity' in Lia's eye / She wants to know 'what's written on the paper'. (**1 mark**)

Grammar, punctuation and vocabulary test answers

1. **1 mark for all three correct**

   I like the **pictures** of **kings** and **queens** best of all.

2. **1 mark**

   Why do some people find Maths difficult?

3. **1 mark for all three correct**

   This morning, **the** sun is shining.

   Let's go for **a** picnic.

   Later, we'll have **an/some** ice cream.

4. **1 mark**

   Adam went to the post office, the bakery, the bank and the petrol station.

5. **1 mark for all three correct**

   You can go into the classroom **and** sit at your tables, **but** if I see anyone running **or** shouting, you will all come out again.

6. **1 mark for both correct**

   Sarah went to the circus with her friends and **they** gave **her** a lift.

7. **1 mark for all four correct**

   How healthy your dinner is → exclamation

   Eat your salad → command

   Vegetables are good for you → statement

   You like cabbage, don't you → question

8. **1 mark for both correct**

He **wore** boots and a warm coat – there **was** snow on the ground.

9. **1 mark**

Mr Sullivan, our next-door neighbour, bought my dad's old bike.

10. **1 mark**

Have you seen the new James Bond film?

11. **1 mark**

I sing and play the trumpet; I love all kinds of music.

12. **1 mark for three correct**

Sentence	Main clause	Subordinate clause
<u>Give me a shout</u> when you've finished.	✔	
<u>If you read the notes,</u> it's easy to play the recorder.		✔
I wore my green wellies <u>because it was raining</u>.		✔

13. **1 mark**

You can find out more later (see page 25).

14. **1 mark**

What a delicious lunch this is!

15. **1 mark**

His trousers don't **match** his shirt.

16. **1 mark**

The tall plant – the one in the hall – needs watering.

17. **1 mark for both correct**

She slammed the door **violently** because she was **so** angry.

18. **1 mark**

The doctor said, 'I hope you feel better soon.'

19. **1 mark**

We have had such a lovely day today.

20. **1 mark for all correct**

Penguins live in the Antarctic where it is very cold. **They lay their eggs on the ice and they swim in the freezing water. They are amazing animals.**

21. **1 mark**

I'm sorry about yesterday – I hope you weren't upset. My **sister's** friend came to visit so I couldn't see you.

22. **1 mark**

As soon as Julia **had finished** her homework, she turned on the television.

23. **1 mark**

It is essential that you reply within one week.

24. **1 mark for both correct**

After they **had eaten**, they left the restaurant.

I always **lock** the door when I go out.

25. **1 mark for all three correct**

   If we're late, we'll miss the beginning of the film.

   When I visit my grandparents, they always let me stay up late.

   The adults cooked lunch **while** the children played in the garden.

26. **1 mark for all three correct**

   Please leave your books **on** the table, make a line **by** the door and walk slowly **to** the hall.

27. **1 mark for both correct**

   The children **were baking** a cake. They **were mixing** the ingredients in a bowl.

28. **1 mark for all three correct**

   The children were frightened → M

   when they heard the scream → S

   they crept into the cave → M

29. **1 mark**

   The lady **who lives next door** is a singing teacher.

30. **1 mark**

   too tired

31. **1 mark**

   Are you sure that cardigan belongs to you? It looks the same as **mine**. Please look in the drawer and see if your cardigan is there.

32. **1 mark for both correct**

   Despite the sea's **calm** appearance, the surfers were afraid that the waves would be **rough** later in the day.

33. **1 mark for each correct; 2 marks in total**

   a) Suggested answer: Find a safe place to cross.

   b) Suggested answer: Do you know how to cross the road safely?

34. **1 mark**

   My friend Katie is 5 feet 6 inches (over 1.5 metres) tall.

35. **1 mark**

   hearing

36. **1 mark for each correct; 2 marks in total**

   a) At the weekend, I washed **the dog**.

   b) In London, **Josie** went to the Science Museum with Uncle Ed.

37. **1 mark**

   Oliver asked me, 'Are you feeling tired?'

38. **1 mark**

   I shall play football.

39. **1 mark**

   I put on my swimming costume and dived into your swimming pool **which** was fairly deep.

40. **1 mark**

   That fair-haired girl is my cousin Meg.

41. **1 mark for all three correct**

   We **ordered** our food, but I **thought** the menu **was** very confusing.

42. **1 mark for each correct; 2 marks in total**

    a) A synonym is a word that has the same meaning as another word.

    b) Suggested answers: realise, understand, recognise

43. **1 mark**

He said, 'You /She can go without me.'

44. **1 mark**

Children's own answers

45. **1 mark for each correct; 2 marks in total**

    a) The mechanic mended our car.

    b) Spanish is spoken by many people.

46. **1 mark**

If I **were** to live in another country, I would choose Italy.

Spelling test answers

1. The fridge was **completely** empty this morning.

2. There is no need to **mention** the party.

3. Most clothes are made by **machines** in factories.

4. If you go out to eat every day, it's not a **special** treat.

5. Lara **received** a confusing email from her teacher.

6. We have a **guest** staying for the weekend.

7. My grandparents love **gardening** in all seasons.

8. Our school had a visit from a **famous** football player.

9. Licking ice cream with your **tongue** makes it last longer.

10. Samuel will do well because he has plenty of **confidence**.

11. **Although** I have no pets, I am an animal lover.

12. The detectives could not solve the **mystery**.

13. Lettie thinks her bedroom is tidy but her mother **disagrees**.

14. When we study **nature**, we understand our planet better.

15. My cat's favourite **position** is sleeping in front of the oven.

16. The play was too long so the director cut some **scenes**.

17. You have gone to a lot of **trouble** to make lunch.

18. Our **neighbour** has lived in the street for fifty years.

19. The box was **considerably** lighter than I expected.

20. There is no **doubt** at all in my mind.

Glossary

abstract noun a noun that refers to feelings, ideas or states that do not exist physically (e.g. 'hope', 'love')

active voice the form of a sentence where the subject does the action (in contrast to the *passive voice*)

adjective a word used to describe something or somebody (e.g. 'red', 'interesting')

adverb a word that gives information about a verb, adjective or another adverb, sometimes formed by adding 'ly' to an adjective (e.g. 'slowly', 'anxiously')

adverbial (phrase) a phrase that functions like an adverb

antonym a word that has the opposite meaning of another word in the same language

apostrophe (') a punctuation mark that is used to show possession or in contractions

article one of the words 'a', 'an' or 'the'

brackets a pair of punctuation marks (), used either side of extra information in a sentence

bullet point (•) a small, round mark used at the beginning of each item on a list in which every item starts a new line

capital letter the form of a letter that is written A, B, C, etc., used at the beginning of a sentence, for example

clause a special phrase that includes a subject and a verb; a clause can be a complete sentence

cohesive device a word such as 'however' or 'moreover', used to link sentences or paragraphs and show the relationship between them

collective noun a noun that is used to refer to a group of things (e.g. 'family', 'team')

colon (:) a punctuation mark that is used, e.g. in front of a list or a part of a sentence that explains something

comma (,) a punctuation mark that is used to divide clauses or items in a list, for example

command a sentence or phrase that tells someone to do something

common noun an ordinary noun that starts with a lower-case letter (e.g. 'table', 'anger', 'air')

comparative adjective an adjective that is used to compare things (e.g. 'longer', 'darker', 'more beautiful')

complex sentence a sentence usually made up of a main clause and one or more subordinate clauses

compound sentence a sentence made up of two independent clauses joined by a co-ordinating conjunction

concrete noun a word for things you can detect with your senses (e.g. 'water', 'arm', 'zebra')

conjunction a word that links two words or phrases together; there are two types: coordinating conjunctions and subordinating conjunctions

consonant a letter of the alphabet that is not a vowel

contraction (*or contracted form*) a word that is made by joining two words but omitting a letter or letters (e.g. 'don't', 'I'm')

co-ordinating conjunction a conjunction that links two words or phrases together as an equal pair

dash (–) a punctuation mark used for example to add extra information in a sentence or to indicate a pause before part of a sentence

definite article the word 'the'

determiner a word that specifies a noun as known or unknown (e.g. 'the', 'a', 'this', 'my', 'some')

direct speech words that are actually spoken by a character in a novel or story

ellipsis (…) a series of dots to show where words have been deliberately left out of a sentence ('ellipses' is the plural)

exclamation a sentence or phrase that begins with 'how' or 'what' and ends with an exclamation mark, used to express strong feelings such as surprise or shock

exclamation mark (!) a punctuation mark that is used at the end of an exclamation

expanded form the full form of a word that is sometimes contracted (e.g. 'do not', 'I am')

formal describing language that is suitable for serious writing such as essays, reports or work

fronted adverbial a word or phrase that acts as an adverb and which goes at the beginning of a sentence (e.g. 'In the end', 'On the other hand')

full stop (.) a punctuation mark that is used at the end of a statement

helping verb a verb such as 'be', 'have' or 'can' that goes with another verb to form different tenses or give different meanings

homophones words that sound the same, but have different spellings and meanings (e.g. 'bear'/'bare')

hyphen a short line used for joining words together (e.g. 'record-breaking', 'flat-screen')

indefinite article either of the words 'a' or 'an'

informal describing language that is suitable for use between friends – e.g. in speech, texts or emails

inverted comma one of a pair of marks ' ' or " ", used in written language for showing what someone said (also called *speech marks*)

irregular describing words that do not follow the usual patterns of words of a similar type

main clause part of a sentence with a subject and a verb; a sentence contains at least one main clause, which makes sense on its own

modal verb a verb such as 'can', 'could', 'may', 'shall', that is used with another verb to express, e.g. probability, permission, ability, advice and obligation

negative a form of a word that means 'no' or 'not'

non-standard English any form of English that is not accepted as a conventional form

noun a word that is used for a thing, person, place, substance, feeling, etc. (e.g. 'table', 'thought', 'energy', 'London')

noun phrase a phrase with a noun as its main part

object the person or thing that has the action of the verb done to them

paragraph part of a text that usually contains several sentences; each paragraph starts on a new line

parentheses a formal word for brackets

passive (*or* passive voice) the form of a sentence where the subject does not do the action, but has the action done to him, her or it (in contrast to the *active voice*)

past perfect the tense that is used to talk about things that happened before the main action started, formed with 'had' and a past tense verb (e.g. 'They had already arrived')

past progressive the tense that is used to talk about things that were happening at a particular time in the past, formed with 'was' or 'were' and an 'ing' verb (e.g. 'We were chatting')

personal pronoun a pronoun that is used to refer to a person or thing (e.g. 'I', 'them', 'it')

phrase a group of words that are grammatically connected

plural a word that shows that you are talking about more than one person or thing (e.g. 'legs', 'churches', 'mice')

possessive pronoun a pronoun that shows who owns something (e.g. 'ours', 'mine', 'yours')

prefix a letter or a group of letters added to the beginning of a word or letters, which alters its meaning (e.g. 'aeroplane', 'illegal')

preposition a word that tells the reader the relationship between things or people (e.g. 'near', 'by', 'under', 'towards')

prepositional phrase a phrase that has a preposition as its head followed by a noun, pronoun or noun phrase

present perfect the tense that shows past events, and uses 'has' or 'have' and a past tense verb (e.g. 'He has gone away')

present progressive the tense we use to talk about things that are happening now, formed with the verb 'be' and an 'ing' verb (e.g. 'I am making bread')

pronoun a word that is used instead of a noun (e.g. 'it', 'they', 'this', 'she', 'mine')

proper noun a name for things like people, places, historical events, organisations, days and months

question a sentence or phrase that asks someone something

question mark (?) a punctuation mark that is used at the end of a question

question tag a short phrase such as 'isn't it?' or 'haven't they?' used after a statement to see if someone agrees with you

regular regular words follow the usual patterns of words of a similar type

relative clause part of a sentence beginning with a relative pronoun, that gives extra information about a noun

relative pronoun a word used to link a clause to a noun or pronoun (e.g. 'which', 'that', 'who')

reported speech an account of what has been said, without using the exact words spoken

root word (or root form) the most basic form of a word

semi-colon (;) a type of punctuation that links two ideas, events or pieces of information

simple past the past tense that is usually formed by adding 'd' or 'ed' to the verb

simple present the present tense that is used for regular events and situations or states that do not change

simple sentence a sentence with one main clause, usually containing a subject, verb and object

singular a word that shows you are talking about only one person or thing (e.g. 'leg', 'church', 'mouse')

speech marks inverted commas

standard English the form of English most widely accepted as the conventional form

statement a sentence that tells you something

subject the person or thing that does the action of a verb

subjunctive a form of the verb used in formal writing to talk about things that should or might happen

subordinate clause a clause that depends on another clause in order to make sense

subordinating conjunction a conjunction that introduces a subordinate clause

suffix a letter or a group of letters added to the end of a word or letters, which alters its grammatical form (e.g. sweet**ness**, driv**er**)

superlative adjective an adjective that is used to show that something or someone has the most of a particular quality (e.g. 'best', 'cleverest', 'most ridiculous')

synonym a word that has the same meaning as another word in the same language

tense the way verbs are used to show the time (past, present or future) that the writer is talking about

word family a group of words that all include a part that is the same or similar, so that the meanings are connected (e.g. 'happy', 'happiness', 'happily')

verb a word that is used to talk about an action or a state (e.g. 'walk', 'happen', 'understand')

vowel one of the letters 'a', 'e', 'i', 'o' or 'u'